A Handbook On Distance Education with Special Reference to Library and Information Science in India

By

Shri Umesha

Dr. Mahesh Mudhol

Shri K.M. Khan

Ess Ess Publications

4837/24, Ansari Road, Darya Ganj,
New Delhi-110002
✆ : 23260807
Fax : 23274173
E-mail: essess@del3.vsnl.net.in
url:http://www.essessbooks.com

First Published 2004

ISBN : 81-7000-375-X

Price Rs.400/-
Ess Ess

Published by :

Ess Ess Publications

4837/24, Ansari Road, Darya Ganj,
New Delhi - 110 002
Phone : 23260807
Fax : 23274173
E-mail : essess@del3.vsnl.net.in
url: http://www.essessbooks.com

Laser Typesetting:

Mukesh Graphics

L-2/8, DDA Market,
Mangolepuri, New Delhi
Ph. : 27924405

Printed at :
Print Line

CONTENTS

List of Tables

List of Figures

CHAPTER 1
INTRODUCTION

"Man is neither more intellect, nor the gross animal body, nor the heart or soul alone. A proper and harmonious combination of all the three is required for the making of the whole man and constitutes the true economics of education"

- Mahatma Gandhi

Education is the process through which man endeavors to pass along to his children his hard-won wisdom and his aspirations for a better world. This process begins shortly after birth, as parents seek to train the infant to behave as his culture demands.'

The term 'Education' in the widest sense may be held to include the whole process of development through which a human being passes from infancy to maturity, gradually adopting himself to his physical and social environment but main importance given to raining the level of culture attained.

Education should create an urge for gathering wisdom and promoting understanding. Knowledge, wisdom and understanding are the ascending and yet durable steps in the ladder of education. Education is a mighty potent weapon for making man and sloping him.

The modern trend of education is to develop a rational individual who should prove to be a self reliant person in every walk of life. It should be an education which would lead him in right direction for proper development of his mind. This can be achieved by wide reading which is sure to lead him to form his independent judgement of the problem facing him.

1.1 ORIGIN OF EDUCATION

The word 'Education' comes from the Latin word 'EDUCARE' meaning 'to dig out'. The primary purpose of education is, therefore to digout or bring out the potential and capabilities of a student (or a person) and not just imparl or accumulate knowledge.

In ancient India the educational system was aimed at building of character, development of personality and preservation of the ancient culture of our motherland. But the whole system underwent a radical change with the arrival of the English people and this resulted in a complete break with the past and even after 54 years of independence we still have to rediscover the roots of our ancient culture. Education should aim at a balanced growth of an individual and insist on both knowledge and wisdom.

1.2 AIMS OF EDUCATION

Education is a life long process. Education aims at preparing the individual for the membership of the society by unfolding all the facts of his personality. Personality is regarded as the sum total of mental, spiritual and physical characteristics of person. The purpose of education is development of life. Every effort of man is towards an existence that which is prosperous, happy, contented and peaceful. The high degree of education all will be able to apply the knowledge to plan for the future. The report of University Grants Commission (UGC) speaks about education in these words, " Education according to the Indian tradition, is not merely a means to earning living, nor is it only a nursery of thought or a school for citizenship".

Education generally involves four stages, they arc learning, practical experience, research and teaching. A.P. Shrivastava says that, learning involves thinking, reading, writing and speaking, what' a man gets from his learning is practical experience. Once he get experience he will mediate or discriminate information simultaneously grabbing information from information simultaneously grabbing information from various sources to become an researcher. Once he succeeds in research he become an expert. Finally he may become a teacher/guide who teaches/guides others this is net outcome is an expert.

1.3 TYPES OF EDUCATION

Education is of two types i.e., the formal education and non-formal education which can build up self confidence in each student, so that he can face the world in a better way after he leaves the institution. On getting into life, he finds a different world, the picture of which had not visualised in his class room nor was be fully equipped intellectually to undertake the new responsibilities and discharge his obligations.

Formal education is deliberately and consciously planned and its curricula are predesigned and goals are predetermined. It comprises direct schooling and tuition intended for pupils of particular age-group.

Non-formal education is offered at convenient place, time and level of understanding or psychological growth of children or adults. Therefore, unlike nor a prescribed course of study. Similarly, it is free from authoritarian outlook and regid rules as well as regulations. It has limited goals and purpose. It is open-ended and non-competitive.

The University system has the formal and non-formal systems leading to that of graduation and above. The "Open University System", or "Distance Education", or "Distance Learning", within the non-formal education system caters to the needs of even employed people. Hence in the recent years it ha taken its momentum in society.

By and large the students in the formal education system are financially supported through the parental encouragement, self-earning and social schemes like merit scholarship and community scholarships. The courses, facilities and services provided by distance education lo distance learners arc considered lo be the area of present study.

1.4 DIFFERENCE BETWEEN FORMAL AND NON-FORMAL EDUCATION

Non-formal education may be defined as the education which lies outside the organisation of formal system of education. Formal system is organised with a specific purpose in all its aspects-staff, equipment, students and the physical plant.

The main emphasis is on teaching while the

non-formal emphases learning and knowing student's needs and interests.

Formal system is full time and subsequential in character, while non-formal may be of any type-correspondence, part-time, own-time and condensed courses.

Formal education is imparted in an educational institution-school or college or university. While non-formal education can be built round all social, economic and cultural institutions such as forms, factories, shops, offices, library, museum, mass media.

Uniformity and regidity from the main features of the formal system while non-formal programme tends to be characterised by the concepts of diversity, flexibility and elasticity.

In the formal system the courses and contents are prefixed by the authorities concerned while in the non-formal system the courses and their contents are determined by the needs, interests, professional requirements and the stage of the learners'

Non-formal education is an arrangement where in flexibility is the key word. The system is an open one with regard to various aspects of education i.e. admissions, curricular, place of instruction, mode of instruction and the time and duration of instruction. Open university, open learning and the correspondence courses are the various examples of such a system.

1.5 CORRESPONDENCE, DISTANCE AND OPEN EDUCATION

In India, the system of correspondence education was introduced at the university level for the first time in the year 1962. We have only recently entered the era of distance and open education.

Correspondence teaching in the strict sense means the imparting of instruction through correspondence. The postal service forms the link between the teacher and the taught and the problems of the students are solved through correspondence.

The two terms correspondence leaching and home study should not be used to synonymous. In correspondence teaching there is some institution or agency which assumes the responsibility of coaching the pupils through different media while home-study in its strict sense means self-study.

Correspondence teaching implies a teaching responsibility on the part of the institution or a person offering the services; while home-study with its emphasis on place of study and it is sometimes interpreted in the restricted sense

Prof. Takwale emphasises the distinction between distance and open education and puts forth the view that distance education is essentially the outcome of modern communication technologies. A well designed network of communication facilities should make it possible for everyone who seeks to acquire knowledge to have access to educational programmes. It is, therefore, desirable to develop open educational systems using distance education methodology to ensure quality of education, extension of educational opportunity and serve large numbers with the diversity of cources that are relevant to the individual and also to societal needs. Distance Education refers to the process of learning in which there is spatial and usually temporal distance between the teacher and learner on the other hand, Open education (or open learning) refers to the process of making learning available to a lerner at a place and time of his/her choice, and at a rate suitable lo the learner.

While discussing distance education in the Indian context Kulandai Swamy (1992) refers to it as the third stage in the evolution of education, the first stage being represented by the Gurukul System of ancient India and second stage by the conventional classroom system. He believes that the distance education system symbolises the transition of education from the stage of craft to the technology.

Distance education system takes care of the planning, development, production, transmission and evaluation of courses and, therefore, they resemble an industrial operation.

The correspondence education, has been quite popular in this country. Lately some of them have designated themselves has Distance Education and Open University System.

The term Distance Education basically emphasis seperation of the teacher and the learner, and planning of educational programmes and material by an educational organisation and use of technical media on a large scale.

The opportunities for part-time education through programmes like correspondence courses should be extended as widely as possible and should also include courses and technology. A committee appointed by the UGC (Mrs. Muley Committee) has gone into the working of the correspondence institutions in the country and has highlighted their dificiencies.

In some of the meetings of the Directors of Correspondence Course also, such issues have been raised. Broadly speaking, they arc:

(i) Correspondence education is looked down upon and is treated as a second calss system of education.

(ii) Most correspondence institutes provide arts and not science courses.

(iii) Most of the offer the same courses which are offered in the formal system. As a result, they have the same rigidities with regard to admission and examinations.

(iv) Most of them use only one medium, i.e. print, and are not multi-media based.

(v) Very few educational institutions in this country make proper resource allocation to correspondence courses. Even the assis tance provided by the UGC is very insignificant and insufficient.

(vi) There is practically no co-ordination among correspondence courses within the country as well as within a state which has led to duplication of effort and wastage.

The heads of correspondence institutes in many universities are not permanent. They do not have much voice in the decision making bodies of the univeristy.

Open education is a term that has been used interchangebly with distance education. Manpower commission described as "arrangements to enable prople to learn at the time, place and space which satisfies their circumstances and requirements".

The main features of Open Universities are:

- They are, like their conventional counter part, autonomous bodies and are free to take their own decisions and formulate their courses.
- They use multi-media for instructional purposes-electronic media is an important component.
- There is a strong student support service.
- The material is prepared by teams of experts.
- Entry qualifications arc flexible and relaxed.
- One can study according to his own place and convenience.
- There is uniformity in the quality of education, i.e. the students have access to the same high quality education.

1.6 OBJECTIVES OF THE STUDY

The objectives of the study are :

- To know the different courses offered through distance education in the country and their services in LIS education in particular.
- To asses the various facilities and services that made available in distance education to distance learners.
- To know the functioning of the Distance Centres at different levels in the country.
- To know the gaps in Distance Learners and Distance Education Centres.

1.7 METHODOLOGY

The following method is used for collecting data and information for the present study.

A large number of records were consulted pertaining to the education, distance education and library science education such as University Reports, UGC Reports, Annual Reports, News Letters, Books etc. in order to collect necessary information for the study.

ersonal visits are also made to some universities, for the purpose of collecting required information. Personal interviews made with some teachers and librarians and necessary information is collected.

1.8 SCOPE OF THE STUDY

The scope of the study though confined to services of the distance education in LIS other aspects like counselling, admission procedure, course material, library facilities etc. have also been studied in a general way.

REFERENCES

1. Shane, Harold G..Education What It Was, Is and Could Be. In: Comptons Encyclopacdia and lact index., Vol. 7. New York: Computer learning company division of Encyclopaedia Britanica, 1986, pp 74.
2. BHATIA, K.K. and NARANG, G.L., Principles and Techniques of Education. Ludhiana : Prakash Brothers, 1974, pp 4.
3. MOHANTY, J., Indian Education in the Emerging Society. New Delhi: Sterling, 1982, pp 136.
4. PALIWAL, M.R., Social change and Education: Present and future. New Delhi: Uppal, 1984, pp 216.
5. Ibid., pp 243
6. Reddy, G. Ram., Distance education: What, Why & How ?. In : B.N.Koul, Bakshish Sing and M.M. Ansari ed. Studies in Distance Education. New Delhi: AIU and IGNOU, 1988, pp 20.

CHAPTER 2

DISTANCE EDUCATION

"We want that education by which character is formed, strength of mind is increased, the intellect is expanded and by which one can stand on one's own feet. Education is the manifestation of the perfection aread in man."

– Swami Vivekananda

Distance Education has great potential to serve the multitude of' eager learners. It will play a major role in providing access to higher education and furthering the concept of life-long learning. In recent years distance education has emerged as a viable alternative to formal education.

There is bewildering variety of nomenclature for this new system of education prevalent in different countries. For example, in Australia it is known as External System, in France Tele-enseignement, in Germany Fernunterricht and so on. In India, it is commonly reffered lo as Correspondence Education, though educationalist belonging to the Open Universities refer to it as Distance Education. It is also called Homestudy, Independent study, External-Study, Off-campus study, Open-Learning, Open-Education, Correspondence-Education etc. are used terms interchangeably.'

Distance Education emerging as one of the effective modes for providing knowledge, skill, education and training to the learners even in remote and far flung areas.

In our country, there arc predominantly two types of institutions which used mode for education and training. They are:

(i) Established Open Universities: Who design, develop, adopt/adapt, translate produce and deliver programmes; and

(ii) Correspondence Course Institutes of Conventional Universities: Under going transformation into distance mode institutions.

2.1 CONCEPT OF DISTANCE EDUCATION

Distance Education, in its present form, originated in the West. In India, University of Delhi was the first followed by Punjab University and others to start programmes in this mode. R.F. Erdos defined it as a "method of teaching in which the teacher bears the responsibility of imparting knowledge and skill to student, who does not receive instructions, orally, but who studies in a place and at distance determined by his individual circumstances". But the most quoted definition of distance education is that of Borje Holmberg (1995). According to him distance education includes "the various forms of study at all levels which are not under the continuous and immediate supervision of tutors present with their students in lecture rooms or on the same premises, but which, nevertheless, benefit from the planning, guidance and tuition of a tutorial organisation".

2.2 DEFINITIONS

Distance Education is defined by Parraton as "an educational process in which a significant proportion of the teaching is conducted by someone removed in place and time from the learner". It is not a way of replacing teachers in schools, but rather a means to support them with high quality materials. Moore (1990) defines distance education or distance learning as "all deliberate and planned learning that is directed or facilitated in a structured manner by an instructor separated in space and/or lime from the learners"

2.3 CHARACTERISTICS OF DISTANCE EDUCATION

Distance Education describe those forms of education in which teacher and learner carryout their essential task apart from one another. Keegan (1993) has identified five characteristics of distance education:

- The involvement of an educational institution or organisation (which distinguishes distance education from private study);
- The use of media (most often print) to unit teacher and learner;
- The provision of a means of two way communications;
- Learning on a individual rather than on group basis;
- From perspective of the institution, the possibility of the economies of scale that go with an industrial form of production (e.g. printing, broadcasting).

In short, distance education is a system of education in which there is no face-to-face relationship between the teacher and the taught, but they are linked through different media as print, radio, T.V. etc. Distance Education provides occasional instruction with faculty, provides for student independence and individualised or off-campus, which is based on students needs.

2.4 SCOPE OF DISTANCE EDUCATION

Distance Education is democratic as well as socialistic in nature. It helps in diffusion of education and equalisation of educational opportunities. In the entire world, the population is increasing so fast that formal means of education cannot keep pace with it. Providing proper educational opportunities to such vast numbers can be taken care of by means of distance education only.

This non-formal means of education has a wide scope for the emerging learning society in general and educationally under developed or developing society in particular. It has message both for life long education as well as for universalisation of education.

Distance Education is an organised provision for learning opportunity on part time basis, outside the time table of formal system of education, covering a person's life time in his own environment, more or less according lo his own perception and at his own time.

The scope of distance education is very large as it is capable of taking in a vast and varied clientic which includes:

- In-service persons who for economic or other reasons had to take up jobs at an early age but are on the look out for an opportunity to improve their educational qualifications.
- Drop -outs who later become motivated to resume their studies.

- Persons in the geographically remote rural areas where there are no institutions of higher learning.
- Retired personnel or the persons near retirement who want to take up studies to keep themselves occupied or to improve their qualification so that they may be able to keep themselves gainfully pre occupied in post retirement period.
- Socially and economically backward sections of the society.
- Persons who are unable to join formal education due to overflow in many educational institutes where admissions are made on merit and for a fixed number of seats.
- Persons who want to learn and cam simultaneously.
- Persons who want to study a subject just for the love of it.
- Handicapped persons.
- Persons who need some additional training in their vocation for updating their knowledge and career advancement.
- Persons, in the affluent societies, having plenty leisure time, persue it as a hobby.

2.5 HISTORY AND DEVELOPMENT OF DISTANCE EDUCATION

2.5.1 Global Scenario

The growth of distance education can be

traced back to the middle of 19th century and the lead in this Field was taken by many European countries such as Germany, England and Sweden. In 1856 at Berlin, for the first time established a school for teaching languages by distance education.

In U.S.A., in 1891, Thomas J. Foster, proprietor and editor of a newspaper, directed the writing of a course of instruction, through correspondence, for the safety of mining workers. Tins later on developed into International Correspondence School of Scronton, Pennsylvania

In England, in 1894, Joseph William Knipe started distance education at a small scale. This later on developed into Wolsey Hall, Oxford.

The first Open University was started in Britain in Milton Keynes, in 1969, which came out to be a great success. It was, indeed, a major breakthrough in the field of education. The success of Milton Keynes Open University resulted in the opening of three more Universities in Western Europe Fern University of Germany, the Spanish university National distance education a distance and Netherland's Open University.

In former USSR, where distance education came under the national policy, this technology played the wonders. In 1989, there were 1,169 distance education courses For the technical studies alone. Out of Five million students in higher education during 1988-89, 40 per cent were the students of distance education system.

In Africa, distance education was mainly aimed at imparting training to the in-service personnel. Now, this system has been fairly spread in Nigeria, Kenya, Tanzania, Ethiopia and Ghana.

Where as in Asia, there has been a phenomenal development of distance education. This development occurred at very high pace during eighties when distance education system made rapid strides in India, Pakistan, Tailand, Sri Lanka, Philippines, China, South Korea, Indonesia and Japan. Most of these countries have adopted the latest innovations of distance education and established Open Universities. In China, primary importance is given to electronic media, where as in other Asian countries, the emphasis is placed primarily an print medium and electronic media arc normally assigned a supplementary or complementary role.

The credit for establishing the International Council for Correspondence Education (ICCE) in 1938, goes to Mr. J. W. Gibson. In the 12th World Conference of ICCE in Vancouver, this organisation was renamed as International Council for Distance Education (ICDE). This ended the long term controversy over the nature of two commonly used terms "Correspondence Education" and "Distance Education"

The Correspondence Education, is restricted primarily to the postal delivery of print material, whereas the term "Distance Education" reflects the multimedia approach to dissemination of knowledge. Correspondence education thus assumed an important role in the total system of distance education.

2.5.2 Indian Scenario

The gradual development and growth of distance education all over the world had its echo and impact in India also. In July 1962, University of Delhi started correspondence courses as a pilot project. These courses were started in the pursuance of the recommendations of an expert committee under the chairmanship of Prof. D. S. Kothari, Chairman, UGC. These courses were assigned to a body called the Directorate of Correspondence Education and Continuing Education.

The successfull experience of Delhi University in conducting this pilot project bearing excellent results set in motion the other universities thinking in the direction of introducting correspondence courses in their respective institutes at different levels. In 1968, the Punjabi University, Patiala was the second University in India to offer these courses. By 1985,31 Universities gave instruction by correspondence at various levels. It has been estimated by UGC that the University system alone provides instruction through distance education to nearly 4 lakh students at various levels in the University structure at a given point of time. This implies that nearly 11 per cent of the total enrollment in the Universities is accounted by distance education.

In India, the system of distance education has passed through three stages:

2.5.2.1 The first stage (Pre-take off stage)

This stage can be identified with the efforts made during the sixties, when only four institutes of Correspondence Education were established, viz., Delhi University (1962), Punjabi University (1968), Meerat University (1969) and Mysore University (1969). The sixties was therefore, a period when the idea of distance education took shape and began to strike roots in the Indian environment. The distance education movement had thus started in India, and was slowly and gradually gathering momentum so that it could enter the take-off-stage.

2.5.2.2 The second stage (Take-off Stage)

During the seventies, nineteen universities started Institutes or Directorates of Correspondence Education and thus a major thrust was provided to distance education in India. The period of establishment of distance education teaching units in these universities arc;

Punjab and Himachal Pradesh (1971), Andhra and Sri Venkateshwara (1972), CIEFL, Hyderabad (1973), Patna (1974), Bhopal, Utkal, Bombay (1975), Madurai-Kamaraj, Jammu and Kashmir, Rajasthan (1976), Osmania and Kerala (1977), Allahabad and SNDT (women's) Bombay (1978), Annamalai and Udaipur (1979). Thus Distance Education got a big push during the seventies. More and more universities look lo distance education as alternative technique of education.

2.5.2.3 The third stage (Drive towards Growth)

The end of seventies, distance education was part of the conventional university system. It had to, therefore, work within the ambit of the procedures of the conventional universities. For the first time in the history of distance education in India, the Government of Andhra Pradesh took up the momentous decision to establish Andhra Pradesh Open University in 1982. Thus an autonomous institution of the level of a university was setup to develop distance education.

At the National level, the Indira Gandhi National Open University (IGNOU) came into being in September, 1985. The chief objectives of this apex institute are:

- To promote Open university and distance education systems.
- To determine the standards of leaching, evaluation and research in such systems.
- To allocate and disburse grants to colleges, whether admitted to its privileges or not, or to any other university or institution of higher learning, as may be specified by the statutes.

Several State Governments have also taken steps towards the establishment of Open Universities in their respective slates. In this category, Kota Open University (KOU), Rajasthan in 1987, Yashwant Rao Chavan Maharashtra Open University (YCMOU), Maharashtra in 1989, Nalanda Open University (NOU), Bihar in 1989, Madhya Pradesh Bhoj Open University (MPBOU),

M.P. in 1993, Babasaheb Ambedkar Open University (BAOU), Gujarat in 1994, Karnataka State Open University (KSOU), Karnataka 1996." These universities are engaged in imparting instruction through the medium of distance education.

At present, there are 10 open Universities in the country (Appendix 1). Besides, 64 Universities are running correspondence courses, leading to different kinds of degrees and diplomas. The share of distance education in the total enrollment which was 11.5 per cent in 1992, had increased 16.5 per cent by the end of 8th Five year plan (1992-97).

The annual total student enrollment in these 10 universities 4,72,102 in the year 2000, with a cumulative enrollment of about 1.3 million. The universities have establishment of a wide network of Regional Centres and study centres for providing student support services. Around the 34,979 academic counsellors are engaged by these universities to provide and counselling services to learners. The Open Universities in India, though few in number, have created an impact on higher education by developing wide range or programe by employing audio-visual technologies in instructional materials and maintaininghigh standards. About 235 programmes with 2146 courses at a different level i.e., Certificate, Diploma, Degree, Post graduate and research arc an offer by these Universities

2.6 THE DISTANCE EDUCATION SYSTEM

A system operates through its components which complement and supplement the operations of each another. The distance education institute under discussion may be conceived to have the following system.

(i) Planning and Management

(ii) Administrative

(iii) Academic

(iv) Delivery System (Teaching Learning Process)

 * Learning Material;
 * Tutors (Human Resources)
 * Learners;
 * Formative Evaluation; and

(v) Evaluation (Summative)

A layout[6] of the Distance Education System is given in Fig.1. It may be noted that there should be an internal consistency among various sub-system should be adequate and timely. The sub-system Planning and Management, Administrative and Academic should serve the sub-system Delivery system in appropriate quantity and quality. The Delivery System and the Evaluation system should be supplied with sufficient quantities of parallel test items and evaluation strategies.. After the sub-system Formal Evaluation, there is a decision box indicating that if the output is not satisfactory, the learner should be provided further training to suit his requirements. In the latter case, the learner should

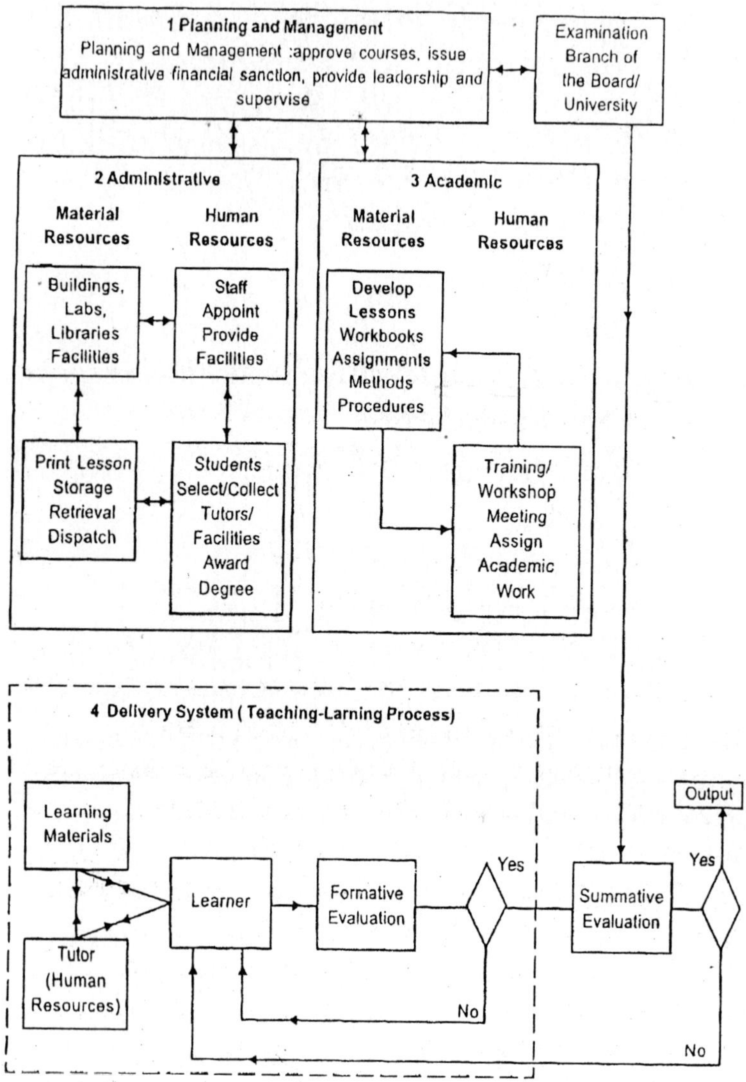

Fig. 1. Distance Education System

receive the remedial training. The Distance Education system postulated by A. Kayeand G. Rumble, the Distance Education system should be analysed in terms of an integrated system of operating, logistic and regulatory sub-systems. The operating system converts inputs into outputs. The main outputs of a distance learning system arc courses and educated people as shown in Fig. 2.

The function of the logistic system is to procure and replenish inputs through activities as purchases and maintenances of equipment. The regulatory sub-system is at the core of the system and facilities the co-organisation of various activities of the institution and relates the organisation lo its environment.

2.7 DISTANCE EDUCATION EVALUATION MODEL

The evaluation model of distance education system consists of three facets. Firstly, evaluation of student's performance; secondly, evaluation of the programmes of distance education on a continuing basis; and thirdly, evaluation of the distance education system itself. The purpose of the student evaluation is to know how much knowledge the student has assimilated from lime lo time and at the end of the term.

The second type of evaluation refers to the formative evaluation. It is also known as the process evaluation. The purpose of this evaluation is to review the working of a programme so as to bring about changes, if needed.

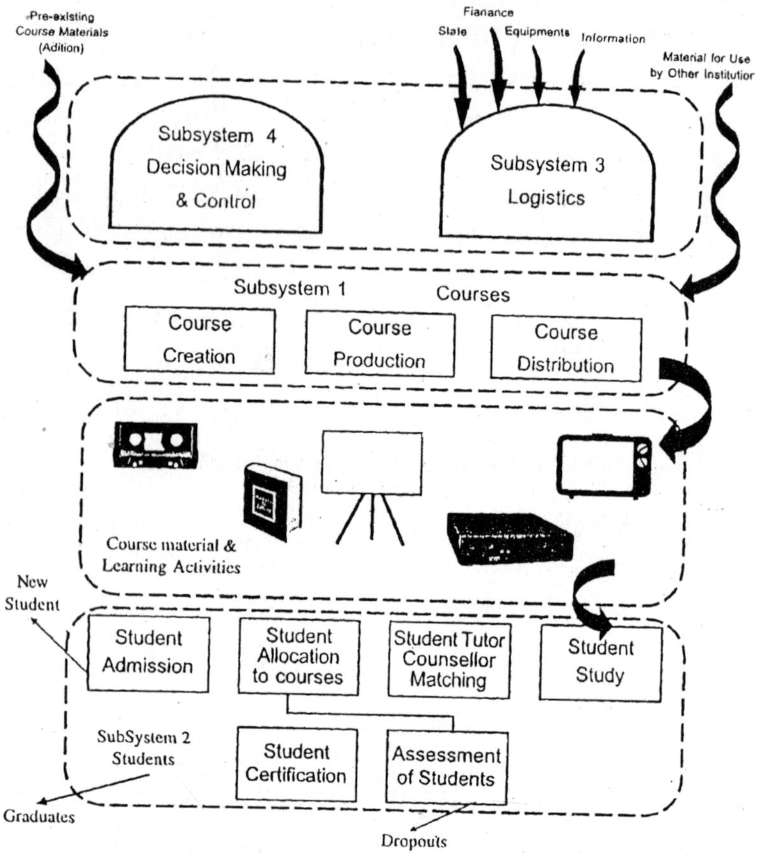

Fig. 2. A Systems view of Distance Education

The third component of evaluation model consists of the sub-system of summative evaluation. Of the different approaches to it, the Rumble's approach is highly popular. He gives four levels of analysis to measure the effectiveness of the higher education institutes. These include:

(i) The response time test;

(ii) The output and input ratio;

(iii) The correctness of output i.e. checking that does it correspondence to the system's goals, needs and demands of the community and students; and

(iv) Cost-efficiency and cost-effectiveness.

A detailed model[8] of these sub-systems and their interrelationship is given in Fig. 3.

It consists of formative evolution, process evaluation and summative or product evaluation. All the three kinds of evaluations are essential to keep the distance education system in a sound state.

2.8 AUTONOMOUS DISTANCE EDUCATION

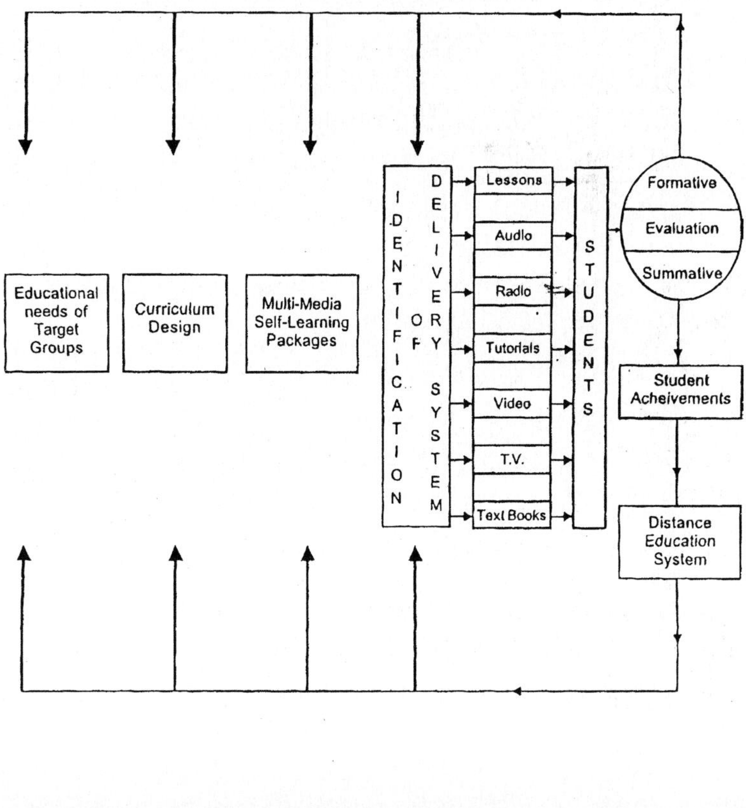

INSTITUTIONS

The establishment in 1969 of the British Open University marked a turning point in the development of distance education, in two ways. Not only was it the first institution designed solely and specifically for distance at degree level, but it was also designed as a multimedia teaching institution, combining print, broadcasting and face-to-face tuition in an integrated manner. Its annual operating budget is approximately 100 million, and it produces 9% of all the undergraduates in Britain in each year. .it a cost of 5% of the National university operating budget, reflecting the high investment/high output potential of technically based teaching.

The Open University's provision of higher adult education, at a distance through the use of technology, has led lo an organisational structure quite different from that of conventional universities. It is thus an excellent example of the structural changes in organisation that are needed for the systematic large-scale application of technology to education.

Since the creation of the Open University, over 25 similar autonomous university institutions dedicated solely to distance education have been established in different countries throughout the world. These are institutions that operate across whole countries, states or provinces. They arc enabled by government lo award their own accreditation, in the form of degrees, diplomas or certificates. They use a variety of media, and usually have large numbers of students. However, large, antonomous distance leaching institutions are by no means the only or even major form of distance education.

2.9 TYPES OF PROGRAMMES OFFERED BY OPEN UNIVERSITIES AND CORRESPONDENCE COURSE INSTITUTES

The Open Universities offer 65 general programmes in liberal arts and the Correspondence course institutes officer 28 of these. The professional/vocational technical programmes offered by the Open universities arc 65 and by correspondence course institutes 191. There are largely related to Management and Computer Education.

2.10 SERVICES PROVIDED BY OPEN AND CORRESPONDENCE INSTITUTES

Student support services for effective learning and resources provided for delivery of programmes are key factors. The same arc summarized in the Table 4.

Open Universities have course materials in Self-Instructional Material (SIM). However, the use of multimedia/multiple media and telecast and broadcast facilities are inadequate except for IGNOU and three state open universities. In view of the priority of the Distance Learning Institutes, both Open Universities and Correspondence Course Institutes should be resources to provide and develop better facilities in the delivery of

Table 1. Services of Open and Correspondence Institutes

Sl. No.	Item	Open Universities	Correspondence Centre Institutes
1.	Learning Materials Print	Most of the Open Universities have Print materials in Self Instructional Material (SIM) format. A few Open Universities have adopted/adapted/translated IGNOU materials as their course materials.	Print Materials of most of the CCI's not in SIM format. Need transformative and revision.
2.	Audio/Video facilities to Supplement the learning	Five Open Univ. viz., IGNOU, BRAOU YCMOU, KOU and MPBOU have good audio facilities. IGNOU BRAOU and YNMOU have adequate Video (A/V) facilities available with other Open Universities are poor and inadequate.	Inadequate A/V facilities being used by CCI's.
3.	Telecast/ Broadcast	Only IGNOU has well developed telecast and broadcast facilities to facilitate learning. YCMOU and BRAOU have launched tele-conferencing and broad casting.	No telecounselling facilities/ broadcast facilities being used by CCI's.
4.	Network of Study centres	Open Universities have good network of study centres.	Organise contact programmes at Headquarters. Inadequate network of study centres.

programmes.

The fact that IGNOU has over 6 lakh students, 44 Regional and 626 study centres, spread all over the country.

2.11 ADMISSION PROCEDURE

The Open universities are offering admission into degree and post graduate courses (PG) even for individuals who do not have any educational qualification. By getting through the entrance or eligibility test, the candidate can seek admission directly into the degree or PG course. A student from a traditional unit has to study and appear for many papers to get through the qualifying examination. But the eligibility tests conducted by open universities cannot evaluated the student's competency to purpose the course. This is much more work in the case of a student seeking admission to PG courses. It is observed that the tests conducted by few universities are very easy and conducted only as a formality to admit more students and in turn, generate more finances.

There is a hue and cry from several quarters of traditional universities on eligibility test. Generally, there are complaints that the test is written not by the candidates by importers as the environment at examination centres is influenced by several factors. This type of activity will have adverse impact on the final examinations. The university officials have lo take necessary steps to check such malpractice.

2.12 COURSE MATERIAL

Comprehensive course material has to be provided lo the learner. It is an uphill task for the universities to get qualitative course material prepared before scheduled time frame. In the process, there is every likelihood of occurance of many lapses and mistakes. It is not possible for any university to revise the course material at short intervals as it works out to be very expensive. On the other hand, at the university education level the universities must be able to provide the latest and updated knowledge. Further, the course material is an important sourse that projects the image of the programme. To provide latest and updated knowledge as well as to correct the mistakes, the open universities should explore and identify the various ways and means of providing accurate and latest information. The universities should make corrections in the course material and send the same to the learner along with the materials. The university can take a help of counsellors, who are spread all over this country/ state with different background. Indentification and corrections of mistakes in course materials is one time process.

The universities should bring out an UPDATE publication (for circulate among the learners) as a supplement to course material. This should contain the latest information/developments in the concerned field as well as the bibliographic details (if possible will) abstracts) of relevant litrature published. This is essential to make this learner to keep abreast of the latest developments in one's Field of study. This can be issued at regular intervals.

Preparation of audio visual (AV) material should be a continous process as they help in providing latest information. Presently, the universities are unable to provide information about the corrections as well as on latest developments.

2.13 ASSIGNMENTS

In IGNOU courses (BLISc) 30% of marks are allocated for assignments and 70% for terminal examinations. Some universities give assignements, but there is no provision for marks/ weightage for completing them. The assignments are of two types, namely (1) Ccomputer Marked Assignments (CMA) (Objective type questions) and (2) Tutor Marked Assignment (TMA). The nomenclature may be different in other university.

The learner is supposed to study the course material and other documents to gain knowledge and also to answer the assignments. It can be observed that the counsellors arc forced to help lo complete CMA in counselling sessions or out side the class room as part of councelling activity.

Tutor marked assignments are corrected by the counsellors, who are generally from traditional colleges/universities. The universities had stipulated guidelines for evaluation and also offering attractive remuneration to the tutors. But unfortunately many evaluators are not following the guidelines and simply give good grades to the students to avoid querries from them. Further, the comments, are not as prescribed by the universities. Hence, it is suggested that the universities should lake up a sample of assignments avalualed by each evaluator and examine how the grades are given and the procedures adopted in evaluation. Also, it would help lo correct the erring evaluators.

2.14 COUNSELLORS

It is essential to select the counsellors who are competent knowledgeable. Unfortunately, in many cases the select is based on paper qualifications and/or lobbying. The local study centres have to play a key role in the selection. But unfortunately it is observed that some of the counsellors neither have subject nor communicative competetive (especially in the context of regional media students). The universities should make it a point to select cousellors having teaching experience as far as possible, especially for PG courses as they constitute the key component in the distance education system and directly interact with the students and help in the learning process. Feedback needs to be taken care of by the authorities. Necessary steps have to be initiated to avoid people who do not contribute towards realisation of the stated objectives.

A small committee consisting of all cast two senior professional in the concerned field with a nominee of the study centre and the university may be constituted for identification of right counsellors.

2.15 COUNSELLING

Generally, the counsellors are asked to do counselling or clear the doubts of the learner in understanding the lessons. But due to traditional educational background they have learners who expect a lecture from the counsellors. The university insists not to resort to lecture method. Further, the students arc not regular in attending counselling sessions as the system does insist an attendance. Unfortunately the counsellor is in a Fix. While the university insists that the student should be encouraged to raise questions, the students generally do not raise doubts as they have not read the course material before attending the class. Of course, several counsellors are adopting via media, that is, by delivering lecturers and trying lo provoke the learner to discuss the- subject.

2.16 LIBRARY FACILITIES

Access to library facilities is important for the students at higher education level. At present the facilities are meagre and the study centres do not provide the books for home reading except in rare cases. The university should do something to extend such facilities. The following methods may help the students to have better access to the relevant sources of informations.

The periodical articles and chapters from books relevant to each course/ paper/topic have to be collected by the library. The list of the same should be circulated to each student. The library must be able to provide at cost price photocopy of the article by the student.

The university should identify the college and university libraries who can come forward to provide the library facilities lo open university students. The student should pay through the university to the concerned college/university a fixed amount towards library fee and library deposit. The university can give guarantee for the books as the student's certificates will be with them. With this college/universities can have a regular income and interest on deposit. The universities can also provide some token amount or reading material to improve the library facilities at such centres.

The Study Centres and the Regional Centres should appoint someone to take care of the library and also to provide services to the users. Presently, in most of the case the books are in accessible lo the students as they arc kept under lock and key. The problem is much more in using the-non-book materials such as video and audio cassettes. Recently, IGNOU evaluation cell has started collecting the data regarding access to such materials.

In addition to the above, there are small and simple problems faced by the students such as non-receipt of material and lack of response for their queries. These problems can be sorted out without any difficulty.

Most of the open universities have recruited teaching faculty in almost all the subjects. Some of the departments have a good number of staff. The universities should ask them to take up in addition to preparing the assignments all the problems relating to their courses. The staff of the departments should continuously and regularly interact with the counsellors to identify the .problems, latest subject information to be incorporated in the course/UPDATE and to gain from their experiences. This is much more essential whenever a new course is introduced. It is also important to interact directly with the students in the presence of the counsellors and study centre staff to identify the problems and solve them. This type of interaction helps the university staffs to gain first hand knowledge about the field situation. It is essential that the concerned staff arc only sent to interact with the students and counsellors. The interaction is much more essential as the study centre staff may not be able to understand the problems.

The learner needs to be regularly provided access to books and other reading materials including multimedia. Every counsellors needs to be provided with a set of books in the concerned program as it helps them to know the contents of various courses of the programme. It will also help them to relate the topics and to decide on the topics to be emphasised in the subject wherever necessary. The universities should Fix the responsibility on the departments and the teachers must be made accountable.

2.17 ROLE OF ACADEMIC, SPECIAL AND PUBLIC LIBRARIES

In India, there is a wide scope for the development of public libraries by enrolling distance learners of Correspondence Institutions and Open Universities as their members. At present there are only eleven States where library legislation is in operation. Most of the Stales have well established, functional public libraries system though formal library legislation has not been enacted. It is evident that a well established public library system can reach every nook and corner of the country.

Resource sharing is the only means to cope up with the tremendous task of providing library and information facilities lo masses the learners by ensuring access lo a wide range of resources already available at various libraries, viz., academic, special and public. This can be possible only through the joint efforts of all existing libraries and by utilising their infrastructural facilities and library resources for longer hours which otherwise would remain idle on the evening and holidays. Library Corners for Distance Learners (LCDL) can be established at Academic and Special Libraries having adequate space, manpower and resources with the help of distance leaching institutions.

The Libraries at the Headquarters and Regional Centres should provide Inter-library loan services (ILL) by making arrangements with various academic as well as special libraries. The Open Universities have their self-instructional materials which have become very popular among students and staff of the conventional universities."

2.18 STUDY CENTRES

The Study Centres arc directly under the control of the university or are linked through Regional Centres to the university. They have a central library for the university staff and libraries at Regional and Study Centres for supporting staff as well as cousellors and students. They provide reading and reference services, facilities to listen to audio cassettes, view to video cassettes and general information service.

The Central Library at the Headquarters combines the features and functions of both an academic library as well as special library. This dual characteristics increases the complexities of library policies regarding the development of collections and provision of library and information services.

2.19 STUDENT SUPPORT SERVICE

Once a programme is launched, a student is attached to a particular study centre where lie is supposed lo gel all types of support services like counselling, library facilities, submission of assignments and its evaluation, watching audio-video programmes, conducting practicals, seminars, teleconference, national telecast programmes, evaluation of assignments etc. Various problems of students both in academic and administrative in nature should immediately we attached so that a learner is motivated to complete his/her programme in time.

2.20 ATTENDANCE

It is not compulsory for distance students. They arc allowed tu write the exams without attending the contact classes and counselling programmes. In some universities 10% of attendance is made compulsory and in some distance programmes also for example BRAOU attendance to contact programmes is compulsory for appearing the examination.[12]

Distance Education may gradually gain more and more importance as the basic and the only alternative solution against the many ills planning the formal systems of education. Every conceivable domain of learning as a necessary integral part of the overall national programme of Human Resource Development may come within its fold so that the formal programmes slowly and stadily are replaced.

REFERENCES

1. Satyanarayana, R., Library and Information Science through Distance Education. Library Science with a Slant to Documentation Vol. 27(3), Sept. 1990. pp 152.
2. Bhaskar Rao, Digumarti *ed.*, Encyclopedia of Education For All. Vol. 1, New Delhi; APH, 1996. pp 257.
3. Kaur, A.S., Managing Distance Education. New Delhi: Deep & Deep, 1996. pp8
4. Jagannathan, Neela. Libraries in Distance Teaching Universities. *In* : M.K. Jain *ed.* Fifty

years Library and Information Services in India. Delhi : Shipra, 1998. pp66.

5. Saroja, G., Information Resource Centres in Distance Education. University News Vol. 39 (38), Sep. 2001. pp 8.
6. Op. cit., Managing Distance Education. pp 33.
7. Ibid., pp 37.
8. Ibid., pp 39.
9. Rousariya, R.B. and Bhushan, Bharat., Institutional model for distance learning in India. University News Vol. 39 (27), July 2001. pp 9.
10. Laxman Rao, N., distance Education in India: Few observations, *In* : U.C. Sharma and M.R. Rawatani ed. Librarianship Today and Tomorrow. New Delhi ESS ESS, 199. pp 84
11. Op. cit., Libraries in Distance Teaching Universities. pp 74
12. Sugatri Devi, K., Curriculum On-Campus and Off-Campus LIS Education programmes in India: A comparative Study. *In* : L.S. Ramaiah et al., *eds.*, Information and society. New Delhi: Ess Ess, 1997. pp 136.

CHAPTER 3

LIBRARY AND INFORMATION SCIENCE EDUCATION THROUGH DISTANCE MODE

"Education is the process of the individual mind getting to its full possible development... It is a long school which lasts a life time"

- Dr. Zakir Hussain

Library and Information Science being a professional programme is intended to develop the skills of a learner in the scientific organisation of the library collections and its timely delivery to the users. The role of library and information professional have totally been changed in the present day society with the application of information and communication technologies.

Distance education can be adopted by individuals who are place-bound and have employment or house commitments which make it possible for them to attend the on-campus LIS education programmes. Being student oriented system it allows a self-paced learning process.'

3.1 OBJECTIVES

Library and Information Science education is basically intended to develop the professional knowledge and skills in the learners. It has the following objectives:

- to meet the lower, middle and higher level manpower needs of the academic, public and special libraries,
- to provide opportunities for career advancements,
- to trace out the foundations of LIS and its characteristics,
- to provide opportunities to earn qualification in the area of LIS to the persons who could not join form stream due to various factors,
- to upgrade and enhance the professional level

of knowledge and understanding of the working librarians who are not having formal qualification,

- to provide self supported and less expensive professional education to the working professionals living in rural and remote places,
- increase self awareness and application of learning to the work place
- produce highly motivated human resources,
- transcends geographical/physical barriers of a learner,
- equip themselves with the managerial skills needed for the strategic management of library and information organisations.

Although the main purpose of LIS programmes through distance mode was to provide an opportunity to the employed professionals only. There has been an increased demand for such programmes from unemployed youths who could not get such opportunity of being admitted in conventional universities to get themselves employed in various library and information centres.

3.2 LIS EDUCATION THROUGH DISTANCE MODE: AN OVERVIEW

Several countries have embarked on distance education system to impart LIS Education, eliminating the tyranny of distance. In the US, as per the survey conducted by Lenox in 1989, there are atleast 26 of the 60 ALA accredited programmes offering distance teaching graduate library education. In fact, the distance LIS education programmes started in the 1970's when the University of Rhode Island offered these programmes the division of LIS at San Jose State University also offers off-site education.[2]

Library Education has also been provided by the College of Library and Information Science at University of South Carolina. Victoria University of Wellington offers post-graduate diploma course in librarianship. The International School of Information Management based at Santa Barbara, California offers only distance learning courses leading lo Master's Degree, via the electronic network, ISIMnet. The University of Missouri's School of Library and Information Science's graduate extension courses are an integral part of Master's Degree Programme in Library Science.[3]

In Canada, the School of Education of Toranto University provides audio-conferenced courses in LIS at graduate level since 1982. Athabasca University, Alberta, distance education programme provide training and certification for staff of small and rural school and public libraries.

In U.K. Haythronwaite has identified eight courses being offered at professional level through distance education. Of these, two courses lead to Master's Degree. On, the Master's Degree Management of Library and Information Science offered by the college of Librarianship of Wales, established in 1985. Second, the M.B.A. in

Information Management launched by the International Management Centre for Buckingham (JMCB) and Association of Information Management (ASLIB). All the other courses available provide training in specific area with some relevance to information work. Jordan Hill college of Education in Glasgow offers post-graduate diploma in Educational Technology, which is of some relevant to Library and Information Scientists.

In China, at present there are correspondence courses offered in numerous centres in which more than 3000 people have enrolled. Leading institutions such as Wuhan University have been authorised lo offer Bachelor's Degree Programme through correspondence. Further, the Television University of China as established a specialist programme in LIS.[4]

Newly industrialised and developing countries in Asia have been rather quick in the adoption of the concept of distance education in their educational development. Hence, institutions like Korea Air and Correspondence University (1972), Allama lqbal University of Pakistan (1974), Sukhothai Thammathirat Open University Thailand (1978), Sri Lanka Open University (1980) and at home the Indira Gandhi National Open University (1985) have been established for the development of education.5

3.3 LIS EDUCATION THROUGH DISTANCE MODE IN INDIA

Library and Information Science (LIS) education has a history of more than hundred years and has the credit of producing millions of Library Information professionals, teachers and researchers. The formal system of LIS education today is squirming under regidity regarding enrollment. The relieve the pressure on formal system and to cater to the increasing demand for the course, the higher educational institutions have been prompted to introduce LIS education through distance mode.[6]

W.A.Borden and A.D. Dickinson initiated the formal course of Library Education in India. Borden established a training course at the Central Library, Baroda in 1911 and Dickinson at Punjab University in 1915. The training school at Punjab University was considered to be the second Library School known in the world, the first being Columbia School. Gradually other universities and library associations started setting up library schools. Madras Library Associations (1929) and Bengal Library Association (1935) started certificate course among the Universities, Madras University under Dr. S.R. Ranganathan took over the Certificate Course from Madras Library Association in 1931. The course was subsequently converted in to Post-Graduate Course of one-year duration in 1937. Post Graduate Courses also started in other Universities subsequently, i.e. Andhra University (1935), Banaras Hindu

University (1941) and University of Delhi (1947). University of Delhi in subsequent years started providing facilities for research leading to Doctorate Degree. It was again the first to start M.Phil courses in 1977.

In addition to formal teaching courses, some universities have introduced correspondence courses at various levels of education. An important development in non-formal teaching is starting of a degree course by Andhra Pradesh Open University (Hyderabad) in 1985. Mohan Lal Sukhadia University (Udaipur) and Kashmir University (Srinagar) provide correspondence education at Certificate level, Punjabi University (Patiala) at Diploma level and Madras University (Chennai) both at Certificate and Degree levels. IGNOU equipped with multi-media instructional system also planned it from 1987.[7]

Distance Education has become an acceptable and popular system in India in last two decades. Offering Library and Information Science training through Distance Education will allow students enrolled in the programme to obtain the initial academic recognised qualifications in the library and information science profession with the minimum of personal dislocation and loss of income.

The growing demand for Library and Information Science education (LIS) through distance learning at Certificate and Bachelor levels, there emerges the need to introduced Master's programme (MLIS). As a matter of fact, there were a number of representations from the working librarians. This demand has to be satisfied as they cannot offered to undergo this one-year full-time course for various regions like leave facility, administrative problems and the financial implications etc. Further, the UGC insisting on Master's qualification to confer the status of teaching faculty to the librarians. Taking these factors into consideration, the Institute of Correspondence Education (ICE), University of Madras has started MLIS Degree course under distance education from 1989 onwards."

3.4 PRESENT POSITION OF DISTANCE LIS EDUCATION

The demands for the each distance learning programme has increased considerably in India. At present, there are 273 universities in our country, out of which 108 universities/colleges/institutions are offering LIS programmes at Certificate, Diploma, Bachelor's and Master's level. " Of these, 74 universities provide Bachelor of Library and Information Science (BLIS) course, 63 universities provide Master's Degree of Library and Information Science (MLIS) course, 15 universities provide M.Phil in LIS course and 50 universities provide Ph.D. in LIS. Besides, Indian National Scientific Documentation Centre (INSDOC), New Delhi and Documentation Research and Training Centre (DRTC), Bangalore provide associateship courses in Information Science, which are equivalent to MLIS degree.[10]

The latest status of LIS courses in Indian Universities are given in Table 2. It shows that the list of universities provide LIS courses through regular mode. The Table 3 shows that there are 35 Open Universities and Correspondence Course Institutes (CCI's) offering LIS programmes through distance/correspondence mode."

3.5 PLANNING LIS PROGRAMMES THROUGH DISTANCE MODE

Library Information Science, being a professional programme, needs careful planning particularly when it is offered through distance mode. The distance learners need to be motivated since it lacks face-to-face class room teaching to complete their programme in time. Therefore designing such programmes and its implementation should be done in a planned manner. The different stages of planning arc:

- Course preparation
- Production
- Maintenance
- Delivery

3.5.1 Course preparation

It is the first and foremost stage of planning because many things are decided at tins stage such as target group, sentence of the programme, marketability, designing course curriculum, objectives and scope, admission criteria, duration, admission fee, medium of instruction, study methodology and other components for each programme.

Table 2. Regular LIS Courses

S. No.	University	Place	State	BLIS	MLIS	M.Phill	Ph.D.
1.	Aligarh Muslim Univ.	Aligarh	U.P.	✓	✓		✓
2.	Amravathi Univ.	Amravathi	Maharastra	✓	✓		✓
3.	Andhra Univ.	Visakhapatnam	A.P.	✓	✓		✓
4*	Annamalai Univ.	Annamalainagar	Tamilnadu	✓	✓		✓
5.	Babasaheb Bhimrao Ambedkar Univ.	Lucknow	U.P.		2 Yr. Course		
6.	Banaras Hindu Univ.	Varanasi	U.P.	✓	✓		D. Litt.
7.	Bangalore Univ.	Bangalore	Karnataka	✓	✓		✓
8.*	Berhampur Univ.	Bangalore	Karnataka	✓	✓	✓	✓
9.	Bharathi Vidyapeeth	Pune	Maharastra	✓			
10.	Bhavnagar Univ.	Bhavnagar	Gujarat	✓			
11.	Birla Inst. of Tech.	Ranchi	Jharkhand		M.Sc. Inf. Sc.		✓
12.	Bundelkhand Univ.	Jhansi	U.P.	✓	✓		✓
13.	Burdwan Univ.	Bardhaman	W.B.	✓	✓		✓
14.	Calcutta Univ.	Kolkata	W.B.	✓	✓		✓
15.*	Calicut Univ.	Calicut	Kerala	✓	✓		✓

S. No.	University	Place	State	BLIS	MLIS	M.Phill	Ph.D.
16.	Delhi Univ.	Delhi	Delhi	✓	✓	✓	✓
17.	Dr. Babasaheb Ambedkar Marathwada Uni.	Aurangabad	Maharastra	✓	✓		
18.	Dr. Bhimrao Ambedkar University	Agra	U.P.	✓	✓		✓
19.*	Dr. Harisingh Gour Vishwavidyalaya	Sagar	M.P.	✓	✓		✓
20.	Gandhigram Rural titute	Gandhigram	Tamilnadu	✓			
21.	Gauhati Univ.	Guwahati	Assam	✓	✓		✓
22.	Gujarat Univ.	Ahmedabad	Gujarat	✓	✓		✓
23.	Gujarath Vidyapeeth	Ahmedabad	Gujarat	✓	✓	✓	
24.	Gulbarga Univ.	Gulbarga	Karnataka	✓	✓	✓	✓
25.*	Guru Ghasidas Univ.	Bilaspur	M.P.	✓	✓		✓
26.	Guru Nanak Dev Univ.	Amritsar	Punjab	✓	✓		✓
27.	Jadavpur Univ.	Kolkata	W.B.	✓	✓		✓
28.	Jai Narain Vyas Univ.	Jodhpur	Rajasthan	✓			
29.	Jamia Milia Islamia	New Delhi	Delhi	✓			

S. No.	University	Place	State	BLIS	MLIS	M.Phill	Ph.D.
30.	Jammu Univ.	Jammu	J & K	✓	✓		✓
31.	Jiwaji Univ.	Gwaliar	M.P.	✓	✓		✓
32.	Kalyani Univ.	Kalyani	W.B.	✓	✓		✓
33.	Karnatak Univ.	Dharwad	Karnataka	✓	✓		✓
34.	Kashmir Univ.	Srinagar	J & K	✓	✓	✓	✓
35.	Kerala Univ.	Thiruvanathapuram	Kerala	✓	✓		✓
36.*	Kurukshetra Univ.	Kurukshetra	Haryana	✓	✓		
37.	Kuvempu Univ.	Shimoga	Karnataka	✓			
38.	Lalit Narayan Mithila Univ.	Darbhanga	Bihar	✓	✓		✓
39.	Lucknow Univ.	Lucknow	U.P.	✓	✓		✓
40.	Madras Univ.	Chennai	Tamilnadu	✓	✓		✓
41.*	Madurai Kamraj Univ.	Madurai	Tamilnadu	✓	✓		✓
42.	M.S. Univ. of Baroda	Baroda	Gujarat	✓	✓		✓
43.*	Mahatma Gandhi Gramo-	Chitrakoot	M.P.	✓	✓		
44.	Mahatma Gandhi Kashi Vidyapeeth	Varanasi	U.P.	✓			

S. No.	University	Place	State	BLIS	MLIS	M.Phill	Ph.D.
45.	Makhanlal Chaturvedi Rashtriya Patrakarita Vishwavidyalaya	Bhopal	M.P.	✓	✓		
46.	Mangalore Univ.	Mangalore	Karnataka		✓		✓
47.	Manipur Univ.	Imphal	Manipur	✓			
48.	Mohanlal Sukhadia Univ.	Udaipur	Rajasthan	✓			
49.	Mumbai Univ.	Mumbai	Maharastra	✓	✓		✓
50.	Mysore Univ.	Mysore	Karnataka	✓	✓		✓
51.	Nagpur Univ.	Nagpur	Maharastra	✓	✓	✓	✓
52.	North Bengal Univ.	Siliguri	W.B.	✓			
53.	North Eastern Hill Univ.	Shillong	Meghalaya		✓		✓
54.	North Gujarat Univ.	Patan	Gujarat		✓		
55.	North Maharastra Univ.	Jalgaon	Maharastra	✓			
56.	Osmania Univ.	Hyderabad	A.P.	✓	✓	✓	✓
57.	Panjab Univ.	Chandigarh	Chandigarh	✓	✓		✓
58.*	Patna Univ.	Patna	Bihar	✓			
59.	Pt. Ravishankar Shukla Univ.	Raipur	M.P.	✓	✓		✓

S. No.	University	Place	State	BLIS	MLIS	M.Phill	Ph.D.
60.	Pune Univ.	Pune	Maharastra	✓	✓	✓	✓
61.	Punjabi Univ.	Patiala	Punjab	✓	✓		✓
62.	Rabindra Bharati Univ.	Kolkata	W.B.	✓			
63.	Rajasthan Univ.	Jaipur	Rajasthan	✓	✓		✓
64.	Rani Durgavati Vishwavidyalaya	Jabalpur	M.P.	✓			
65.	Sambalpur Univ.	Sambalpur	Orissa	✓	✓		✓
66.	Sampurnanad Sanskrit Vishwavidyalaya	Varanasi	U.P.	✓			
67.	Sardar Patel Univ.	Vallabh Vidyanagar	Gujarat	✓	✓	✓	✓
68.	Saurashtra Univ.	Rajkot	Gujarat	✓			
69.	Shivaji Univ.	Kolhapur	Maharastra	✓	✓	✓	✓
70.	S.N.D.T. Women's Univ.	Mumbai	Maharastra	✓	✓		
71.	South Gujarat Univ.	Surat	Gujarat	✓	✓	✓	✓
72.	Sri Krishnadevaraya Univ.	Anantapur	A.P.	✓	✓	✓	✓
73.*	Sri Venkateshwara Univ.	Tirupati	A.P.	✓	✓	✓	✓

S. No.	University	Place	State	BLIS	MLIS	M.Phill	Ph.D.
74.	Swami Ramanand Teerth Marathwada Univ.	Nanded	Maharastra	✓	✓		✓
75.	Tilak Maharashtra Vidyapeeth	Pune	Maharastra		✓		
76.	Tilak Manjhi Bhagalpur Univ.	Bhagalpur	Bihar	✓	✓		
77.	Utkal Univ.	Bhubaneswar	Orissa	✓	✓		✓
78.	Vidyasagar Univ.	Midnapore	W.B.	✓	✓		✓
79.	Vikram Univ.	Ujjain	M.P.	✓	✓	✓	✓

(* These Universities provide LIS education through both regular and distance modes)

Table.3. Distance LIS Education.

S. No.	*University*	*Place*	*State*	*BLIS*	*MLIS*	*M.Phill*	*Ph.D.S.*
1.	Allagappa Univ.	Karaikudi	Tamilnadu	✓			
2.*	Annumalai Univ.	Annamalainagar	Tamilnadu	✓	✓		✓
3.	Awadesh Pratap Singh Univ.	Rewa	M.P.	✓			
4.	Barkatullah Univ.	Bhopal	M.P.	✓	✓		
5.*	Berhampur Univ.	Berhampore	Orissa	✓	✓	✓	✓
6.	Bharathidasan Univ.	Tiruchirapalli	Tamilnadu	✓	✓	✓	✓
7.	Calicut Univ.	Calicut	Kerala	✓	✓		✓
8.	Dr. B.R. Ambedkar Open University	Hyderabad	A.P.	✓	✓		
9.*	Dr. Harisingh Gour Vishwa-vidyalaya	Sagar	M.P.	✓	✓		✓
10.*	Guru Gasidas Univ.	Bilaspur	M.P.	✓	✓		✓
11.	Hyderabad Univ.	Hyderabad	A.P.	✓			
12.	Indira Gandhi National Open University	New Delhi	New Delhi	✓	✓		✓
13.	Kakatiya University	Warangal	A.P.	✓			

S. No.	University	Place	State	BLIS	MLIS	M.Phill	Ph.D.
14.	Karnataka State Open University	Mysore	Karnataka	✓			
15.*	Kurukshetra University	Kurukshetra	Haryana	✓	✓		✓
16.*	Madurai Kamraj Univ.	Madurai	Tamilnadu	✓	✓		✓
17.*	Mahatma Gandhi Gramo-daya Vishwavidyalaya	Chitrakoot	M.P.	✓	✓		
18.*	patna University	Patna	Bihar	✓			
19.*	Sri Venkateswara Univ.	Tirupati	A.P.	✓	✓	✓	✓
20.	Yashwantrao Chavan Maharastra Open Univ.	Pune	maharastra	✓			

(* These Universities provide LIS education through both regular and distance modes).

Course Curriculum/Structure having both theoretical and practical components should meet the expected requirements equivalent of the programme. At present, four programmes are offered through distance mode i.e., Certificate, Diploma, Bachelor's Degree and Master's Degree in LIS. At certificate level, the emphasis is on (a) functions and services of libraries, (b) organisation of library materials, (c) records of library. The practical components are in the form of assignments, practical, work-books etc. The duration varies from six months to one year.

Diploma in Library Sciences (DLIS) focuses on library and society, classification and cataloguing, bibliography and reference, library organisation and preparation of assignments records etc. The duration of course varies from one year to two years.

Bachelor's Degree in Library and Information Science (ULIS) is of one year duration and the course curriculum is designed taking in to consideration the broad aspects of library organisation, management, information sources, information service, computer application, classification, cataloguing etc. supported by practical component.

Master's of Library and Information Science (MLIS) is an advanced level programme of one year duration and the structure of the curriculum is of little advance than BLIS programme. The MLIS programme of Indira Gandhi National Open University (IGNOU) is more technology oriented giving much emphasis on Information and Communication, Information Sources, Systems, Programmes, Information Processing and Retrieval, Information Institutions, Services and Products, Information Management, Information Technology and its applications in Libraries and Information Centres.

The medium of instruction of all these programmes is English. Students are allowed to appear term-end examination in English or Hindi and in few cases their own regional languages.

3.5.2 Production

It means making both the print and non-print educational resources available to distance learners admitted to each programme. Students are expected to get self-instructional print material, programme guide, assignments, work-books or practical records, other reference material, audio-video cassettes, organising teleconferencing programmes etc. Faculty members are responsible to produce these course material and make it available to the admitted students.

3.5.3 Maintenance

It is the period i.e. updating of course material, preparation of assignments and programme guide, audio-video programmes etc. Although the printed course material once produced is good enough for 5-7 years, it needs to be updated. The assignment questions vary every year. Instructions and addresses are changed frequently. Orientation programmes for counsellors are conducted at different intervals to acquaint them with the course contents and other instructions essential for students. Counsellors at Study Centres directly interact with the students and they try to clarify the doubts and solve problems.

3.5.4 Delivery

The success of programme depends much on its implementation and delivery mechanisms. The programmes are activated in the Study Centres which are the nerve centres between the university and the students. The delivery of the programme is through print material, counselling, library facility, audio-video programmes, national telecast, teleconferencing, compulsory computer practicals and seminars etc. With the help of the counsellors, students clarify their doubts, make use of library to prepare their assignments, watch audio-video programmes and satellite based teleconference programmes, submit tutor-marked assignments etc. and ultimately appear for term-end/final examination.[12]

3.6 CURRICULUM DESIGN

3.6.1 Training to be linked with practice

The curriculum design should be related to the basic requirements of the library profession. It not only aids the librarian to cope with the developments in the library environment but enhances the ability of the librarian also. Library

Science departments need to adapt their curriculum design in accordance with the market potentiality. There must be a relation between the library science curriculum and library practice.

3.6.2 Components of the curriculum

A curriculum in librarianship is made up a several component parts; courses in general culture, practical work, visits to libraries and documentation centres, on-the-job training and end-of-course thesis or report. The course should involve both advance study and research Continuing education for specialised courses is carried out by course materials supplied by library science departments, seminars, workshops and training by library associations.

3.7 COURSE CURRICULUM

The Design the first and foremost step of offering this programme. This needs to be carefully planned and the learning outcomes in terms of understanding, knowledge, application and skills of the distance learners should be reflected by this curriculum.

The curriculum for BLIS comprise:

1. Library and Society or Library and Community or Sociology of Libraries.
2. Library Management.
3. Library Classification Theory and Practice.
4. Library Cataloguing Theory and Practice.
5. Bibliography and Reference Sources or Information Sources.

6. Information Services or Documentation and Information Systems and Services.
7. Computer Basic and Application (included in Annamalai, IGNOU and Madras syllabi).

A conspicuous difference in curriculum of study is that three universities have included computer basics at BLIS level (Appendix III). Further, three is little variation in the titles of the modules. The process of study for the MLIS comprises:

1. Information Processing and Retrieval (Theory)
2. Information Processing (Practice)
3. Communication and Information Systems
4. Library Information Systems Management
5. Research Methodology
6. Application of Computer to Information Storage and Retrieval
7. Elective-Academic Library System.
8. Bibliometric (Annamalai)
9. Preservation and Conservation of Information Materials (Madras)

With an exception to the eight paper, other paper/models are similar in the MLIS programme of Annamalai and Madras Universities (Appendix IV).[12]

Application of Information Technologies in the Libraries and Information Centres shall enable the learners to develop his/her computer skills for its effective organisation. These include:

- Library Automation or Computerisation of In house operations,
- Database design and searching using readily available software packages,
- searching of CD-ROM bibliographic database,
- preparation of on-line search strategies and searches of databases, multimedia application libraries,
- organising information resources available on internet etc.

3.8 STANDARDS AND NORMS

Distance Education Council (DEC), setup under the IGNOU act, is a statutory authority entrusted with the responsibility of promoting, co-ordinating and maintaining standards of Open and Distance Education System in the country. DEC has initiated a number of activities to fullfil its objectives by establishing various quality assurance mechanisms. One of these mechanisms is to develop appropriate norms and guidelines for offering programmes in various fields and their delivery through distance mode.

As a part of this endeavour, the DEC constituted an expert committee, developed and finalised a document on "norms and standards for library and information science programmes (BLIS, MLIS) through distance mode". The document serves as a guidelines for offering BLIS and MLIS programmes through distance mode by open universities and correspondence course institutes. Norms and Standards are relating to curriculum design, eligibility criteria, admission/ selection procedure, duration, student intake and class size, measure of a course or programme, faculty, learning resources, student support services, delivery mechanisms, evaluation, physical facilities and equipment, library, computer facilities, monitoring and system evaluation etc."[14]

3.9 ELIGIBILITY CRITERIA

The Criteria for admission to the courses varies from one university to another. It is shown in the following Table 4.

3.10 METHODS OF TEACHING

In distance LIS programmes, the students are always at a distance from the teacher. There will not be any direct communication between the teacher and the learner. However, to avoid these limitations, the Open Universities and Correspondence Institutions are conducting counselling and contact classes as a regular feature at selected Study Centres. Both theory and practical subjects will be explained to the students in these classes. Further, teaching in distant mode has been established through assignment evaluation. The teacher evaluates the assignments and through his comments imparts learning techniques to the students.

In other modes of teaching distance LIS programmes are through audio-video methods.

Table 4. Eligibility criteria for admission in to LIS courses

Sl. No.	Name of the Univ.	Courses offered	Qualification	Experience
1.	Annamalai (TN)	BLISc	Graduate	Not required
		MLISc	BLISc of a recognised university	- do -
2.	BRAOU (AP)	BLISc	Bachelor's Degree	Regular and substantive experience of one year in any type of library.
3.	IGNOU (New Delhi)	BLISC	Bachelor's Degree	2Yrs. of experience in a recognised library
		MLISc	BLISc degree from any recognised university or its equivalent	

Sl. No.	Name of the Univ.	Courses offered	Qualification	Experience
4.	Kakatiya Warangal (AP)	BLISc	Graduate	Not required
5.	Kota Open Univ. (Rajasthan)	BLISc	Graduates on Non-Graduates with 5 Yrs. of experience	
6.	Madras Univ. (TN)	BLISc	Bachelor's Degree	Not required
		MLISc	BLISc of the same or any recognised Univ.	- do -

However, the study material applied is the main source for the distance learner.

3.11 TEACHING HOURS

In distance LIS programmes, the Open Universities are Correspondence Institutions are organising contact and counselling classes which provide face to face relationship between the students and teachers and provides the student to clarify his doubts in the subjects. For example, BRAOU is conducting contact classes on every second Saturday and two Sunday's in the month. Besides it has a schedule of compulsory contact programmes for 10-15 days having 8 hours duration for a day. Madras University is conducting one month contact and counselling classes during summer vacation i.e. May and June, Annamalai University also organising contact classes of 45 days duration.[16]

It is an accepted fact that distance education has made a considerable progress in the area of Library and Information Science. However, there is still need to make it more qualitative and practical. There is an urgent need to introduce and continue the process of quality improvement in the teaching/learning of Library and Information Science under distance education environment on continuous basis. The ground realities of the present higher education system indicate that quality improvement is essential and unavoidable system indicate that quality improvement is essential and unavoidable not only for the survival of distance education system but also for facing the major changes and challenges of today and tomorrow in the field of Library and Information Science teaching under distance mode.

REFERENCES:

1. MARY, F. Lenox., Distance Education: Report of survey of off-campus/ Extension courses in graduate Library Education Programmes Accredited by the American Library Association. JELIS Vol. 31 (1), Summer 1990. pp 68
2. JAMES, S. Healey., Distance Library Education. Library Trends Vol. 39 (4), Spring 1991. pp 424
3. VARALAKSHMI, R.S.R. Distance Education in Library and Information Science. In.: A.A.N. Raju et al. *eds.* New Vistas Library and Information Science. New Delhi: Vikas, 1995. pp370
4. NINGZHOU and LANLIN., Fourty years of development of Library and Information Science Education in China. JELIS Vol. 31 (2), Fall 1990. pp 166
5. SATHYANARAYANA, R,, Library and Information Science through Distance Education. Library Science with a Slant to Documentation Vol. 27 (3), Sep. 1999. pp 152
6. Op cit.. New Vistas Library and Information Science, pp 372
7. DATTA, Baidyanathi and DAS, A.K., Higher

Education in Library and Information Science in India. ILA Bulletin Vol. 37 (1), March 2001. pp 25

8. GAGADHARA RAO, P. and RAMESH BABU., Recent Trends in Education for Library and Information Science in South India. New York: AP, 1990. pp 181

9. SAMANTHARAY, M. and RATH, Pravakar., Library and Information Science through distance mode in India: an overview. In: M.N. Malwad et al. *eds*- Towards the New Information Society of Tomorrow: Innovations, Challenges and Impact. New Delhi: FID, 1998. pp II-136

10. Op cit., ILA Bulletin, pp 26

11. Ibid., pp 26

12. Op cit., Towards the New Information Society of Tomorrow: Innovations, Challenges and Impact, pp II-139

13. Op cit., New Vistas Library and Information Science, pp 374

14. Distance Education Council (IGNOU). Norms and Standards for Library and Information Science Programme (BLIS, MLIS) through Distance Mode, New Delhi: IGNOU. 1997

15. Op cit., New Vistas Library and Information Science, pp 374

16. SUGATHRI DEVI, K., Curriculum On-Campus and Off-Campus LIS Education programmes in India: A comparative study. In: L.S. Ramaiah et al, *eds*., Information and Society. New Delhi: Ess Ess, 1997. pp 136.

CHAPTER 4

USE OF MULTIMEDIA IN DISTANCE EDUCATION

"The highest education is that which does not merely give us information but makes our life in harmony with all existence."

– **Rabindra Nath Tagore**

In the modern age of knowledge explosion, population explosion and scientific and technological advancement, the distance education is the only remedial measure that enables every citizen to participate effectively in the development of the country. The new technology is not capable of overcoming the barriers that distance presents, but also changes the very nature of the instructional process. It is technology that made the move from correspondence to distance education possible.

The credibility enjoyed by distance education today is mainly because if its multimedia approach. Media climates the problems of distance and carries education to the door steps of the learners.

The multimedia approach not only multiplies class rooms and teachers but also creates enthusiastic environment for the learners in distance teaching.

4.1 MEANING OF MULTIMEDIA

The term "Multimedia" is formed by the combination of two words 'Multi' and 'Media'. Multi refers to many i.e. at least two. Media is the plural form of the medium.' Medium can refer to storage, transmission, communication, representation, presentation, input interaction and perception, meaning that it can refer to different levels of abstraction. Multimedia can be defined as an integration of text, graphics, audio, video disks, video tapes, T.V. etc.

4.2 NEED FOR MULTIMEDIA

Multimedia is aimed at meeting the demand for better access to and presentation of information. The uniqueness of Multimedia lies in its ability to present rapidly a variety and quality of information to meet and needs of different types of users. In the present world, selecting the crucial data is extensive and overwhelming task it is more so in the ease of education and training because multimedia provides a new dynamic environment for instructors, students and others in presentation of work materials more appropriately.

4.3 ADVANTAGES OF MULTIMEDIA

The advantages of multimedia are:

- they facilitates diverse learning objectives,
- they contribute lo specific learning objectives,
- they motivate learners psychologically,
- they help learners, monitor the information input,
- they help learners involved,
- they increase student concentration,
- they accommodate individual needs, and
- they extend the role of a teacher.

4.4 TYPES OF MULTIMEDIA

The multimedia used in open universities/ distance education as well as in institutes of distance learning in India and abroad. We classify them in two types:

(i) Print media; and

(ii) Non-print media

4.4.1 Print Media

Print media are the backbone of all universities and distance education institutions. It is the form of printed self-instruction text arc used as the core media all over the world.

The latest development in printing technology, material is used being brought out with beautiful covers, and catchy captions. In the words of Holmberg, "By for the most important medium in distance education courses is printed word. This applies to conventional correspondence study, as well as to highly sophisticated multimedia presentation like courses of open universities".

The unique feature of IGNOU, print materials is due to the involvement of the team of experts preparing each course keeping in view the interest of the target audience.2

Print materials can be used in any setting without the need for sophisticated presentation equipment. They are instructionally transparent; non threatening because reading is second nature to most students; easy to use, reviewed and referenced; easy to reedit and revise; and cost and time effective.'

4.4.2 Non-print Media

Non-print media is the technologies used by researchers with a large measure of success in the area of non-print media include the following.

(i) Radio and Television

(ii) Telephone
(iii) Audio/Video cassettes
(iv) Video Text
(v) Computer
(vi) Internet
(vii) Satellite

4.4.2.1. Radio and Television

Radio and Television are broadcast-based approach, information is imparted to the students via radio or television broadcasts. These are the two supporting media of distance education.

The advantage of the radio is that all over the world it is within the reach of the common man, and can be carried from place to place easily.

Some of the Directorates of Correspondence Courses in our country broadcast the lessons to supplement the print materials for their distance learners at fixed times. In Andhra Pradesh Open University (APOU), it is used for six hours a week. IGNOU radio broadcast arc also on the air presently from AIR Hyderabad, Bombay and Shillong, every Monday, Tuesday, Wednesday and Thursday from 7.00 to 7.20 A.M."

Television is more effective medium than radio for spreading education because the language of T.V. is rich, powerful and expensive. T.V. lessons are entertaining as well as attractive. The teacher can be seen and heard and his demonstrations and examples can be assimilated more quickly and more easily through television

Television has democratised education. The disadvantaged group of learners living in remote and rural areas of the country get the same quality of education as their counterparts in urban areas.

The IGNOU started telecasting its educational programme on national network from May 20, 1991 on Mondays, Wednesdays and Fridays from 6.30 A.M. to 7.00 A.M. Though T.V. has several advantages over print materials and Radio, it is not within the reach of common man as the sets are very expensive. Further, lack of adequate transmission facilities and dissatisfaction with the time slot available are some of the factors responsible for using the television sparingly.5

We have a 24-hour educational channel-Gyan Darshan-as part of the national repertoire, Gyan-Vani-the radio co-operative-to remove the remoteness through the use of communications technologies. Though the responsibility of running these has been essentially entrusted to IGNOU, this is attributed to the team culture, re-emphasises the greater needed for collaboration of networking.6

4.4.2.2 Telephone

Telephone is a very effective means of communication. It offers two ways interactive communications across distance i.e. people can talk to each other, discuss and ask questions. But in our country this is unlikely to be considered as to medium in distance education.

4.4.2.3 Audio/Video Cassettes

Thought of as a more effective medium than radio or television, the audio/video cassettes can be played and replayed at home by the learner at his/her will. The audio/video cassettes produced for each course by IGNOU are kept at all study centres and regional centres. Students are advised to go to the nearest Study Centres to avail of audio/video programmes facilities when they visit Study Centre for counselling.

4.4.2.4 Video Text

It is one of the latest technologies. It makes home television sets to function like a computer terminal and retrieve text information and graphics from a remote database. It gives much wider access to information and much wider case with which new concepts and ideas can be transmitted, but today videotext is quite expensive. It will take pretty long time for it to be used in distance education in India.

4.4.2.5 Computer

It is computer-based approach implies use of computer to impart education to home-based students via. electronic mail, voice-mail, computer-conferencing and other techniques.

Computer-mediated learning has been a new development being witnessed in educational communication. The mass teaching system has become virtually impossible without computer. Computer is a very good tool to improve the process of teaching and learning. It is of tremendous use for teaching and learning in diverse situations.

Computer-based instruction includes a broad range of application. The major classification of computer application for distance learning are 'Computer Assisted Instruction and Computer Management Instruction'.7

4.4.2.6 Internet

It is the largest, most powerful computer network in the world. It encompasses 1.3 million computers with internet addresses that are used up to 30 million people in more than fifty countries. As more colleges, universities, schools, companies and private citizens are connected to the internet either through affiliations with regional not-for-profit network or by subscribing to information services provided for-profit companies, more possibilities are open for distance educators to overcome time and distance to reach students.

Internet has opened the facilities for web-based training. Delivering training via internet is a key tool to meet all these requirements and visual class rooms or virtual campus is a consequence of this web-based training. Through a dedicated network of computers we can bring in teachers live from different locations."

The easy availability of computers and world-wide internet has brought about significant changes in learning-teaching strategies. In U.S.A. and Canada, every student, has an E-mail account and has either a computer of his own or has easy access to the university computer system. This has solve to the great extent the problems of students and teachers interaction.

The present electronic communication system has made the interaction much easier and essentially less costly. With the access to internet, distance educators and their students can use;

- Electronic Mail (E-mail)
- Bulletin Boards and
- World Wide Web (WWW)

The WWW and Web browsers have made the internet a more user friendly environment. The ability to integrate graphics, text and sound in to a single tool means that novice users do not have to struggle with such a steep learning curve. In addition organisations and individuals can create home pages on their own computers or to pages created by others on different computer system.

4.4.2.7 Satellite

It is the glamorous medium in distance education. It is used for communicating over long distance. More channels for both radio and television are possible because if the satellite. The satellite and television network offers a powerful medium for the dissemination of knowledge, cultural programme and development information. Satellite instructional television experiments have been made in Andhra Pradesh, Rajasthan, Bihar, Orissa, Karnataka, Gujarat, Maharastra, Uttar Pradesh and Madhya Pradesh;

are covered under the Indian National Satellite (INSAT) service from 1983." UGC Educational Programmes for high school and undergraduate students are very popular. The programmes for transmitted via INSAT have really created a dynamic country wide class room not only for students but also for teachers and educated public from 1994 onwards.

Indira Gandhi National Open University (IGNOU) started teleconferencing in 1995 in collaboration with Indian Space Research Organisation (ISRO), using Training and Development Channel (TDC) of INSAT 2B Satellite. Teleconferencing is a virtual class room situation where student can interact with the faculty of school at New Delhi. Presently oneway video and two way audio facility through teleconferencing is provided to 16 Regional Centres, 3 state Open Universities and 2 remote Study Centres.[10]

4.5 COMPONENTS OF MULTIMEDIA

4.5.1 Text

Text is found in most of the printed documents. Text is the basis for word processing programmes and is predominantly used in multimedia programmes. Text is still a quick way to spread information is given in Fig.4.

4.5.2 Graphic Images

Graphic images generally mean a "Still" image, viz., photographs, on-line drawing, or graphs. They play an important role in the presentation of data of any work. Visual oriented materials and pictures arc powerful means to illustrate information either or paper or on computer graphic files are always large and occupy more storage space in computer then text files.

4.5.3 Animations

Animations refer to a moving picture or videos. The animations arc powerful communicators and more useful for illustrating concepts that involve movement. These concepts are difficult to illustrate using photographs and more difficult to explain using text. Animation files require much more storage space than graphic files involving single image.

4.5.4 Sound

Sound can substantially reinforce our understanding of information presented in other ways. It is powerful and useful tool to provide information to users which otherwise is not possible using any other method.

4.5.5 Interactive Links

Interactive links that integrate the whole programme giving the user away to interact with the programme and cause things to respond in a certain way. It is the interactive nature of multimedia that takes care of everything to provide information to users.

4.6 IMPACT OF MULTIMEDIA IN DISTANCE EDUCATION

The National Policy on Education (1986) has stressed the use of media in education in the following terms "modern technology must reach out to the most distant areas and the most deprived sections of beneficiaries simultaneously with the areas of comparative influence and ready availability".[11]

Multimedia is the most valuable tool to support distance education and overcome the problem of illiteracy and semi-literacy.

The Open University system envisages the use of video and computer technologies which ultimately will revolutionised the instructional system. The very names of some popular Open Universities of the world, such as Japan's University of Air, Chaina's Radio and Television University signify the increasing influence and utilisation of modern mass communication technology in distance education.

The IGNOU adopted the policy of using new technological device to support the printed materials. Andhra Pradesh Open University uses different media to support the print media in an integrated form. It has a separate production wing to produce audio-video lessons. The radio lessons are broadcast from AIR, Hyderabad 'B' Station in them morning and during night.[12]

4.7 METHODS OF TEACHING IN DISTANCE MODE LIS EDUCATION PROGRAMMES

- Study Material
- Personal Contact-Programmes (PCP)
- Assignments
- Audio/Video lessons.

4.8 APPLICATION OF MULTI-MEDIA IN DISTANCE EDUCATION IN LIS PROGRAMMES

1. User friendly nature of Multimedia-with its various components like text, sound, animation-will guide the distance learner in understanding the theoretically part of the subjects efficiently and easily.
2. Computer conferencing and those developments which involve interaction with other fellow student could have great value in breaking down the isolation of the lonely and long distance learning.
3. Practical training is very effective with the help of Computer Assisted Instruction (CAI) and Computer Aided Learning (CAL). Certain databases are an excellent example for a databank which the student can teach himself/herself to use.
4. The distant student can easily participate in seminars and discussion through teleconferencing and audio conferencing, as it is possible to see the faces of the other participants. It is now possible to purchase

small computer packages explaining subjects in a simple and clear manner. Such packages can be used again and again by many students.

5. Virtually libraries will help the distance learner to actually feel library tours and involve the students in library functions.
6. Knowledge testing, with the help of CD ROM's available the students can test their knowledge by interacting with the computers.[12]

The success of Distance Mode LIS Education programmes depend largely on the use of alternative media available. The cost must appear to be higher, but judicious utilization of available resources should create a hardware and software base for the extensive use of those technologies in future.

REFERENCES:

1. KUMBAR, Mallinath and BIRADAR, B.S., Multimedia Technology and its impact on Education. In: A.A.N. Raju et al., *ed.*, Information Technology and its impact on LIS Education and Library Management. New Delhi: Delta, 1997. pp96
2. HAIDER, Quseemuddin., Use of Multimedia in Distance Education. In: Zeenath Shafi S. *ed.*, Information Technology in Higher education. New Delhi: AIU, 2000. pp64
3. lbid., pp 64

4. Ibid., pp 65
5. Ibid., pp 67
6. GARG, Suresh and Panda, S., WWW and Distance Education. University News Vol. 39 (4), Oct. 2001. pp 1
7. SHARMA, A.K. and SAKSHENA, D.N., Role of media in Distance Education. *In*: K.B. Powar and Veena Bhalla., Quality Assurance in Distance Higher Education. New Delhi: AIU, 1999. pp 101.
8. GHOSH, C.K., The evolution of Distance Education Methodology: From Print medium to on-line training. University News Vol. 3 9(1), Jan. 2001. pp 6
9. Op cit., Quality Assurance in Distance Higher Education, pp 103
10. Op cit., Information Technology in Higher education, pp64
11. SUGATHRIDEVI, K., Multimedia and Distance. Mode LIS Education Programmes. In: Sathyanarayana B. et al. eds.. Information Technology: Issues and Trends, Vol. I. New Delhi: Cosmo, 1998. pp 1 19
12. Ibid., pp 122

Chapter 5
Epilogue

"Education is a liberating force, and in our age it is also a democratising force, cutting across the barriers of cast and class, smoothing out inequalities imposed by birth and other circumstances."

– Rabindra Nath Tagore

In the words of Fred Jevons, Distance Education should no longer be written off as second best. It has a different pattern of advantages and disadvantages from campus-based education but it is not intrinsically inferior... Distance education has some advantages which should be recognised more widely. Easier access; independent learning opportunities, a more intimate interface with employment, better quality controls over course materials, the possibilities of cummulative in; edagogic quality; the staff development effect and under certain circumstances lower costs.

The medium of distance education is to serve as a valuable tool in any educational system and play a permanent part as a parallel strategy to the regular system, it should have a strong feedback system. Feedback, though difficult to organise, is the only way of initiating dialogue between the teacher and student in a system of distance education.

Distance education, may not be an ideal educational environment for LIS, but emerging as a response to a genuine need of unemployed youth for job-oriented courses and for continuing educational opportunities to in service library professionals. Hence the need of the day is to maintain the standard of the course, the responsibility for which vested with UGC panel on the LIS education, LIS educator participating universities and IATLIS. They have to initiate action in this regard. The LIS education is not a once-for-all affairs, and the under graduate period is but the first phase of a continuing process. Therefore, the foundation for an LIS professional should be strong enough for future developments.

The distance LIS education programmes provide an excellent opportunity for the interested students who arc unable to attend the campus programmes because of their personal reasons.

Distance education programmes in the field of LIS have to go a long way in India. Open universities and Correspondence course institutes need to build up their infrastructural facilities and more student support services. This is the only way to develop the professional skills of the distance learners. Moreover, to bring quality in these programmes, particularly in an information society, the authorities, policy makers and faculty members in LIS should emphasize on providing more facilities to distance learners interested in developing, multimedia educational resources, application of computer and communication technologies, so that the teaching/learning courses will be more interactive, effective and efficient.[1]

The distance learners need more multimedia instructional packages rather than a few printed lesson. Multimedia interactive teaching and learning system makes learning more interesting and effective for the learners.

The present study reveals that distance education in LIS are not quite satisfied with the functioning of this system. Widespread dissatisfaction is prevailing among them, with regard to the student support services. As far as the other variables are concerned, they arc just moderately satisfied. All this indicates that there exists a large scope of improvement in the present state of distance education system in LIS.

The success of distance mode LIS education programmes depend largely on the use of alternative media available. The limitations may be over grown by popularly organising the multimedia into a well defined instructional strategy. Initially the cost might appear to be higher, but judicious utilisation of available resources should create a hardware and software based for the extensive use of those technologies in future.

- Work experience in libraries have to be made compulsory for entry in to the course. Then only a more relevant curriculum, suitable to the particular needs of in service students can be deviced and implemented.
- To have more contact classes with emphasis on practicals.
- Dispatching of reading materials in time.
- To make one year apprenticeship compulsory after MLISc to overcome the variations in course contents and methods of teaching etc. This solves the problems of insufficient practical knowledge.
- Provision of library with lending facility at study centres.
- As the distant-learner depends mainly on study material supplied, the course contents

should be revised atleast once in a five years.

- The electronic media available should be used in addition to the personal contact programmes to teach the distance students; and
- There is no shortage of study materials for distant learners but they should have an understanding of basic principles which will enable them to use classification, cataloguing, and bibliographical tool to the full extent. Therefore, emphasis on practical component is essential. The ideal curricular programmes should reflect the purpose i.e., to train the profession for skills which is the principal component of the curriculum. Hence a adequate opportunity for field setting has to be provided for learning professional skills. Submission of a project after an apprenticeship of three to four months in a recognised library may introduced.
- The process of offering LIS through Distance Education must be reviewed fourth with, as the majority of the intake of students are freshers disguising themselves as working.

Some remedial measures as may be needed are suggested:

- The LIS distance schools have the responsibility to provide library facilities to help students have access to additional reading. This means the study centres need to be adequately equipped.

- The reading materials since from the major input, revision and updation have to be regularly taken up. The quality of contents and readability also need proper care.
- The system should also include as a compulsory provision, practical training/field work/apprenticeship so that the students are exposed to live LIS environment. Similarly, there must also be insistence on records and assignments so that the students are made to work and learn on their own and acquire fairly a good amount of skills and knowledge.[2]
- Equally important is the admission based on better selection/enrollment criteria. A certain minimum standard at the professional study and capability must certainly be insisted upon.

Distance education provides an excellent opportunity for LIS programmes to continue to be directly involved in the education of practitioners. Through the development of instructional packages, tele-conferences, satellite delivered classes, and generally improved communication among all the players, this system of education could become an intellectual neighbourhood of new ideas and services.

REFERENCES:

1. SAMANTHARAY, M. and PRAVAKAR, Rath., Library and Information Science Education through distance mode in India: an overview.

In: N.M. Malwad et al. *eds.*, Towards the new information society of tomorrow: Innovations, Challenges and Impact. New Delhi: FID, 1998. pp II-138

2. RAMESH BABU, B,, Distance Education in LIS: Some observations. In: M.V. Venugopal et al., ed. Vistas in Library Information Systems and Networks (A Festschrift to Prof. S.M. Tripathi). Agra: Y.K., 1999. pp 159.

BIBLIOGRAPHY

1. AGARWAL, S.P., Directory of LIS Education in-India: Compendium on Library and Information Science Study in India. New Delhi: Reliance, 1996.

2. AGGARWAL, J.C., Theory and Principles of Education: Philosophical & Sociological Bases of Education. New Delhi: Vikas, 1999.

3. AMARANATH RAL, Distance Education Open Learning vs Virtual University Concept. Delta: Authors, 2000.

4. ANAND, Satyapal., University Without Walls: The Indian Perspective in Correspondence Education. Delhi : Vikas, 1979.

5. Association of Indian Universities Handbook on Library and Information Science. New Delhi: AIU, 1997. pp 69

6. BEST, John W., Research in Education. New Delhi: Prentice Hall, 1977.

7. BHASKARA RAO, Digumarti., ed., Encyclopaedia of Education For All: The World Conference, Vol. 1. New Delhi :APH, 1996.

8. BHATIA, S.K., Directory of Universities and Colleges of India: with introduction on universities of SAARC countries. New Delhi: Reliance, 1999.

9. BHATNAGAR, S., Distance Education: A System under stress (An in-depth study of the Indian Institute of Correspondence courses). New Delhi: Concept, 1997.

10. BORAH, Swapna., *ed.*, Distance Education. Delhi: Amar, 1998.

11. BROPHY, Peter., eds.. Libraries Without Walls 2: The delivery of library services of distant users. London: L.A., 1998.

12. CHANDER, N. Jose., Management of Distance Education. New Delhi: Sterling, 1991.

13. COREA, lswari et al., ed.. Encyclopaedia of Information and Library Science, Vol. 3. New Delhi: Akash Deep, 1993.

14. ELLIOT, Geoff., Video Production in Education and Training. London: Croom Helm, 1984.

15. FERGUSON, John., Open University from Within. London: University Press, 1975.

16. GUPTA, Pawan, K. and PAWAN, Usha., Library and Information Science Current Trends in India. Jaipur: RBSA, 1986. Pp 171

17. HOLMBERG, Borje., SEWART and KEGAN., Distance Education: International Perspective. London: Routledge, 1988.

18. INAMDAR, N.B. and RAMAIAH, L.S., ed.. National Policy for Universities Libraries in India: Problems and Perspectives. New Delhi: Concept, 1989.

19. Indira Gandhi National Open University (IGNOU), Student Handbook and Prospectus for BLISc and MLISc. 2002.

20. ISAAC, Dorothy., et al. *ed.*, Academic Libraries: Role in the National Development. Madras: T.R., 1993.

21. ISAAC, K.A. and DEVARAJAN, G, *ed*, Libraries in Distance Education, Distance Education

and Libraries. New Delhi: ESS ESS, 1989.

22. ISAAC, K. A., and DEVARAJAN, G., *ed..*, Libraries in Distance Education. ESS ESS: New Delhi, 1990.

23. JAIN, M.K„ Fifty years of Library and Information Science in India. Delhi: Shipra, 1998.

24. KAUR, A.S., Managing Distance Education. New Delhi: Deep & Deep, 1996.

25. KAWATRA, P.S., ed., World Encyclopaedia of Library and Information Science, Vol. New Delhi: Crest, 1994.

26. KEEGON, Desmond., Foundations of Distance Education. London: Croom Helm, 1986.

27. KENT, Alien., ed., Encyclopaedia of Library and Information Science (ELIS), Vol. 52. New York: Marcel Dekkar, 1993.

28. KHAN, Inayat., ed., Teaching at a Distance. Delhi: Amar, 1989.

29. KOUL, B.N., SINGH, Bakshish and ANSARI, M.M., ed., Studies in Distance Education. New Delhi: AIU & IGNOU, 1988.

30. KUMAR, P.S.G. and VASHISHTH, C.P., ed., Library and Information Science in India, New Delhi: Sterling, 1992.

31. KUMAR, P.S.G., ed.. Library and Information Science in India, Through Distance Learning: A Case study of BLISc Programme of APOU, 1997.

32. LIMBADRI, R., Distance Education: A Critical Appraisal. New Delhi: AIU, 1999. pp 12
33. LYNDEN, Frederic, C. and CHAPMAN, Elizabeth, A., Advances in Librarianship, Vol. 22. San Diego: Academic, 1998.
34. LYNDEN, Frederic, C. and CHAPMAN, Elizabeth, A., Advances in Librarianship, Vol. 23. San Diego: Academic, 2000.
35. MADE., Course material on Communication Technology for Distance Education. New Delhi: IGNOU, 1992.
36. MALHOTRA, S.P., Distance Education Problem and Perspectives. Kurukshetra : Kurukshetra University, 1998.
37. MALWAD, N.M., et al., eds.. Towards the New Information Society of Tomorrow: Innovations, Challenges and Impact. New Delhi: FID, 1998.
38. MOHANTY, J., Educational Broadcast, New Delhi: Sterling, 1984.
39. MOHANTY, Sunil Behari., Non-formal education. Allahabad: chugh, 1985.
40. MOLENDE. Michael., HEINICH, Robert., and RUSSEL, James, D., Instructional Media and the New Technology of Instruction. New York: John Wiley, 1982.
41. MOONIS, Raza., Higher Education in India: Retrospect and Prospect. New Delhi: AIU, 1991.
42. NANDA, V.K., Theory of Distance Education, New Delhi: Anmol, 1997. pp 1

43. NIGAM, B.K., and KAUSHIK, Vijay Kumari., *ed.*, Management and Evaluation of Distance Education. New York: Kanish, 1996.

44. NYBERG, David., *ed.*, The Philosophy of Open Education. London: Routledge & Kegon Paul, 1975.

45. PALIWAL, M.R., Social Change and Education: Present and future. New Delhi: Uppal, 1984.

46. PERRY, Walter., Open University. Hertfordshire: The Open University Press, 1976.

47. PFLUNG, Bernd., Self Education: A gandtion perspective. New Delhi: Cyan, 1996.

48. PFLUNG, Bernd., Self Education: A Grand Perspective. New Delhi: Cyan, 1996. pp I

49. PILLAI, C.R. and NAIDU, C.G., Economics of Distance Education: The IGNOU Experience. New Delhi: IGNOU, 1997.

50. POWAR, K.B. and BHALLA, Veena., ed., Distance Education: Concepts. New Delhi: AIU, 1999. pp 5

51. PRASHER, R.G., Library and Information Science: Parameters and Perspective. New York: Concept, 1997. Pp 88

52. RAJU, A.A.N., et al. *ed.*, Information Technology and its impact on LIS Education. Delhi: Delta, 1997.

53. RAJU, A.A.N., et al., *ed.*, New Vistas in Library and Information Science. New Delhi: Vikas, 1995.

54. RAJU, A.A.N., LAXMAN RAO, N., and SUDARSHAN RAO, S., *eds*.. Fifty Years of Library and Information Science Education in India (XV IATLIS National Seminar, Mysor), 1997. pp 154.

55. REDDY, Ramachandra, G., *ed*., Open University the Ivori Towers Thrown Open. New Delhi: Sterling, 1998.

56. RAMAIAH, L.S., et al., fid., Information and Society. New Delhi: ESS ESS, 1997.

57. RAMAIAH, L.S., Images and Perceptions in Library and Information Science. New Delhi: ESS ESS, 1998.

58. RATHORE, H.C.S., Management of Distance Education in India. New Delhi: Ashish, 1993.

59. REDDY, Vishwanatha, K., Tele-Education and the class room: The Indian Experience in Distance Education interface. Hyderabad, Dr. BRAOU, 1994.

60. REITMAN, Sandford W., Education, Society and Change. Bostan: Allyn & Bacon, 1981.

61. RENGARAMANUJAM, P., Reflections on Distance Education for India. New Delhi: Manak. 1995.

62. RUMBLE, G., The Planning & Management of Distance Education. London: Croom Helm, 1986.

63. SAKSENA, Gopal., Television in India: Changes and Challenges. New Delhi: Vikas, 1996. pp 17

64. SARAMAJI, P., Distance Education. New Delhi: Sterling, 1984.

65. SATHYANARAYANA B, et al., *ed.*, Information Technology: Issues and Trends, Vol. 1. New Delhi: Cosmo, 1998.

66. SATYANARAYANA RAO, M., Quality Assurance in Distance Education. Hyderabad: BRAOU, 1995.

67. SATYANARAYANA, B,, et al., £41., Multimedia: Its Application in Library and Information Science. Chennai. T.R., 1998. pp 57

68. SATYANARAYANA, P., and SESHARATNAM, C., Distance Education: What? Why? How?. Hyderabad: Booklinks, 2000.

69. SEN, B.K., ILA Bulletin Vol. 37 (1), March 2001. pp 25

70. SHAFI, Zeenath, S., *ed.*, Information Technology in Higher Education. New Delhi: AIU, 2000. pp 64

71. SHAH, A.B., and SHUSHEELA, B.H.A., *ed.*, Non-Formal education and the NAEP. Delhi: Oxford University, 1980. pp 3

72. SHARMA, K.D., and SHARMA, D.V., ed., Open Learning Systems in India with special reference to school education. New Delhi: Allied, 1993.

73. SHARMA, U.G., and RAWTANI, M.R., Librarianship Today and Tomorrow. New Delhi: ESS ESS, 1997.

74. SINGH, U.K., and SUDARSHAN, K.N.,

Broadcasting Education. New Delhi: Discovery, 1996. pp 3

75. SINHA, R.P., *ed*.. Inequality in Indian Education. New Delhi: Vikas, 1997.
76. TONY, Bates A.W., Technology, Open Learning and Distance Education. London: Routledge Studies in Distance Education Roulledge, 1986.
77. UNESCO Newsletter Vol. 10(3), New Delhi: UNESCO, Sep. 2001.
78. UNIVERSITY GRANTS COMMISSION., Report. 2001.
79. WATSON, K., Education in the Third World. U.S.A: Croom Helm, 1982.
80. YOUNG, Michael., et al,, eds.. Distance Teaching for Third World. London: Roultedge & Kegan Paul, 1980.

APPENDICES

APPENDIX I

TEN OPEN UNIVERSITIES

1. Dr. B.R. Ambedkar Open Universities (BRAOU)
2. Kota Open Universities (KOU)
3. Nalanda Open University (NOU)
4. Yashwantrao Chavan Maharastra Open University (YCMOU)
5. Madhya Pradesh Bhoj Open University (MPBOU)
6. Dr. Babasaheb Ambedkar Open University (BAOU)
7. Karnataka State Open University (KSOU)
8. Netaji Subhas Open University (NSOU)
9. U.P. Rajarshi Tandon Open University (UPRTOU)
10. Indira Gandhi National Open University (IGNOU)

APPENDIX II

NUMBER AND NAMES OF PAPERS AT CERTIFICATE LEVEL

1. Library Management
2. Reference Service & Bibliography
3. Classification & Cataloguing Theory
4. Classification Practicals
5. Cataloguing Practicals
6. Book selection and Information Sources

Kakatiya University

1. Library Organisation & Management
2. Information Sources & Services
3. Classification & Cataloguing Theory
4. Classification Practicals
5. Cataloguing Practicals
6. Assignments (covering reference questions, compilation of bibliography and arrangement of entries in cataloguing)

Madras University

1. Theory (covering Library Organisation, Reference Service, classification and Cataloguing)
2. Practical (covers Library Classification & Cataloguing)

APPENDIX III

LIST OF PAPERS AT BACHELOR'S LEVEL

Andhra Pradesh

Dr. B. R. Ambedkar Open University

1. Library and Society
2. Library Management
3. Library Cataloguing Theory
4. Library Classification Theory
5. Documentation and Information Services
6. Bibliography, Reference Sources and Services
7. Library Cataloguing Practice
8. Library Classification Practice

S.V. University

1. Library and Society
2. Reference and Information Sources and Services
3. Library Classification Theory
4. Library Classification Practice
5. Library Management
6. Library Cataloguing Theory
7. Library Cataloguing Practice
8. Introduction to Computer
9. Records

Kakatiya University

Papers 1 to 7 same as in S.V. University

8. Special Librarianship

Madras and Annamalai Universities

1. Library and Society
2. Library Management
3. Library Classification Theory
4. Library Classification Practice
5. Library Catalogue Theory
6. Library Catalogue Practice
7. Information (Secondary) Sources
8. Information Services
9. Introduction to Computers

Note: The different open universities may be contacted regarding the list of Papers, Admission Procedures etc. requesting them to send the prospectus and other details.

APPENDIX IV

LIST OF PAPERS AT MASTER'S DEGREE

Madras University (1988-94)

1. Information processing and retrieval
2. Information processing (Practice)
3. Communication and information systems
4. Library and information systems management
5. Research methodology
6. Application of computers to information storage and retrieval
7. Academic library system
8. Preservation and conservation of information materials

Annamalai University

Papers 1 to 7, same as in the madras University (1988-94) Paper 8: Bibliometrics

Madras University (from 1995-onwards)

1. Introduction to information science
2. Information sources and services
3. Information storage and retrieval
4. Library classification and cataloguing practice
5. Information centres planning and management
6. Information Technology
7. Research methodology
8. Academic libraries